THE HOLY SPIRIT EXPLAINED

CRYSTAL LOVE

EDITED BY
NICOLE QUEEN

Copyright © 2025 by Crystal Love

All rights reserved. Published in the United States by Vision Publishing House, LLC.

ISBN: 979-8-218-87201-4
LCCN: 2025924760

Vision Publishing House
support@vision-publishinghouse.com
www.vision-publishinghouse.com

This book is established to provide information and inspiration to all readers. It is designed with the understanding that the author is not engaged to render any psychological, legal, or any other kind of professional advice. The content is the sole expression of the author. The author is not liable for any physical, psychological, emotional, financial, or commercial damages, including, but not limited to special, incidental, consequential, or other damages. All readers are responsible for their own choices, actions, and results.

No part of this book may be reproduced in any form or by any electronic or mechanical means, including information storage and retrieval systems, without written permission from the author, except for the use of brief quotations in a book review.

Reproduction of text in whole or part without the express written consent by the Author is not permitted and is unlawful according to the 1976 U.S. Copyright Act.

*To every believer learning to live between Heaven and earth.
You were chosen for this generation.
May these words awaken your identity, ignite your purpose, and remind you
that you were never meant to walk alone.*

You live in two worlds to reveal one Kingdom.
"On earth as it is in Heaven."

— Matthew 6:10

CONTENTS

Introduction		xi
1.	The Day of Man	1
2.	God's Creation & Formation	11
3.	Empowered to Take Dominion	25
4.	God Uses Systems	33
5.	How It All Began	45
6.	God's Divine Plan	55
7.	God's Divine Order	65
8.	The Comforter	81
9.	Predestination	91
10.	Life in God's Garden	107
11.	Revelation & Relationship	123
12.	Chosen to Live in Two Worlds	135
13.	A Clean Slate	151
14.	The Full Expression of the Holy Spirit	165
	Bibliography	199
	About the Author	203
	Also by Crystal Love	205

INTRODUCTION

The Holy Spirit Explained is a book that is designed to help readers understand who the Holy Spirit is and how He plays a crucial role in our lives. This is a book that is not only for those who are saved, but also for those who need hope and direction in their lives that will lead to Salvation.

The Holy Spirit is often misunderstood, and this book aims to clear up any confusion and provide insights into the power and importance of the Holy Spirit. The journey of discovery that led to the creation of this book was through personal experiences. I will dive deeper into the role of the Holy Spirit and how the person of the Holy Spirit has affected my life.

We experience the comfort and exhilaration that comes with knowing that we have a life assistant. With the Holy Spirit by our side, we never have to go through life alone without direction. God's plan is the best and only all-sufficient plan that will work beyond human abilities. The Holy Spirit is an integral part of that plan.

The goal is to help readers understand the Holy Spirit's role in guiding their lives and leading them towards God's plan. Through the Holy Spirit, we can connect with God more intimately, understand His will, and receive guidance on how to live our lives. *The Holy Spirit*

INTRODUCTION

Explained also acknowledges the difficulties that people face in life. It recognizes that life can be challenging, and that people often need guidance and comfort during these times.

According to Hosea 4:6, "My people are destroyed for lack of knowledge. Because you have rejected knowledge, I will also reject you, and you shall be no priest to me. Because you have forgotten the law of thy God, I will also forget thy children."

Due to ignorance, many people have gone down paths that caused distraction, committed terrible crimes, and even experienced premature death, sickness, and so on. This grieves my heart, and this is simply a characteristic of the Holy Spirit—the Holy Spirit grieves. However, God never intended for these things to happen, which is why He gave us His Word.

CHAPTER 1
THE DAY OF MAN

When God finished making man, that sealed the deal for creation. I don't know if you quite understand what that means. That means God is bringing resolution to some things in our lives, and we are going to see the results at the last hour.

Our expectancy on the things that were promised in the Word of God and the foreseen knowledge of our personal destinies have to stay in the forefront. We cannot allow the present disappointments of what is happening in the natural sense to deter us away from what God has revealed in the spiritual realms.

He prepared for man to soar and prosper on earth prior to His arrival, which should be very comforting to us as His children. We have a Father that has a plan for us—a life for us to live that has been predestined. *Predestined,* according to the Oxford Languages Dictionary, means determined in advance by divine will or fate. The Greek word for predestined (*proorizo*) means to decide, mark out, or determine beforehand.

I believe that if we knew the importance of God making a promise to us—knowing that He will not go back on His promise—that should be enough for us to hold on and to hold fast to what

He says and reveals. But because of the anxiousness of mankind and the proclivity that we have to be impatient (which is a reason why God has given us the fruit of the Spirit, one of which is patience and another being long-suffering), these two combined together in perfection and stewarding well will help us to wait on the Lord.

You would think for some of us that all we need is a word from the Lord, knowing the nature of God. But sometimes a word heard one time is not convincing, because everything we see that's going on right now does not look like or reflect what God said and what He actually showed you.

This is why we have dreams and visions of what's to come—so that we can be encouraged to know that what you see is not permanent. And God does not want us to feel like we are alone in the wait. That's why He gave us the person of the Holy Spirit through His Son Jesus, who He is, to live in us.

This ensures that the path we take leads us straight to what He says. If we did not have the Comforter on the inside to help us walk through life, then many of us would never reach the promise.

Jesus said it Himself:

> *"Nevertheless I tell you the truth; It is expedient for you that I go away: for if I go not away, the Comforter will not come unto you; but if I depart, I will send him unto you."*
>
> — JOHN 16:7 (KJV)

> *"Nevertheless I tell you the truth. It is to your advantage that I go away; for if I do not go away, the Helper will not come to you; but if I depart, I will send Him to you."*
>
> — JOHN 16:7 (NKJV)

> *"But in fact, it is best for you that I go away, because if I don't,*

the Advocate won't come. If I do go away, then I will send Him to you."

— JOHN 16:7 (NLT)

Here we have three translations of Jesus saying: *"It is expedient... it is to your advantage... it is best for you..."* that He goes away. Because if He does not, the Comforter, the Helper, the Advocate—will not come to you. The actions of all translations are: *"will not come unto you... will not come to you... won't come."* But if He departs, if He goes away: *"I will send Him to you"* (the Holy Spirit).

The word *to* indicates direction or destination. This shows movement toward a place, person, or thing. So, why would the departing of Jesus cause the Holy Spirit to come? And why did Jesus feel the need to tell this to His disciples?

1. Jesus was here on an assignment.

His time here was limited but purposeful. Imagine being in the physical form with Jesus, witnessing these healings and miracles, and now having to adjust to life without these manifestations, in fear that things in your life would change. Many heard of the promise of a Savior, and here He was—showing up on the scene—and then leaving after only three years of ministry. They may have thought that it was over for them and that life would go back to normal. But little did they know that their journey in life was about to begin. The beginning of a God-filled, Holy Spirit–led life was going to lead to the accumulation and development of other disciples.

2. God was never leaving the throne room of Heaven.

He is the overseer of it all. Though He could have done so, why would He, when that was not His role? We can read throughout the Bible that His role has been, is, and was fulfilled.

> *"In the beginning God created the heavens and the earth."*
>
> — GENESIS 1:1

God is the reasoning behind the seen and the unseen.

> *"For in Him all things were created, things in heaven and on earth, visible and invisible."*
>
> — COLOSSIANS 1:16–17

He is a God of justice who established and upholds the laws of the Kingdom in the earth.

> *"So then, the Law is holy, and the commandment is holy, righteous, and good."*
>
> — ROMANS 7:12

He is our Shepherd, and He guides us into all truth. He is our Savior and Redeemer.

> *"For God so loved the world that He gave His one and only Son, that everyone who believes in Him shall not perish but have eternal life."*
>
> — JOHN 3:16

God is the Judge of the entire world and the King of kings who rules over everything.

> *"For God will bring every deed into judgment, along with every hidden thing, whether good or evil."*
>
> — ECCLESIASTES 12:14

He is the Father of Comfort.

> *"For you did not receive a spirit of slavery that returns you to fear, but you received the Spirit of sonship, by whom we cry, 'Abba! Father!'"*
>
> — ROMANS 8:15

This is why it is so important to develop an intimate relationship with our Father through the Holy Spirit, who is our Comforter and Counselor (John 14:26). Sometimes we think that we are responsible for how things go in our lives, but Scripture declares otherwise:

> *"For I know the plans I have for you, declares the LORD, plans to prosper you and not to harm you, to give you a future and a hope."*
>
> — JEREMIAH 29:11

> *"For we are God's workmanship, created in Christ Jesus to do good works, which God prepared in advance as our way of life."*
>
> — EPHESIANS 2:10

God is taking us from slavery to sin to freedom in righteousness. The righteousness of God is afforded to us by the person of the Holy Spirit, who walks us through sanctification throughout our lifetime.

In the person of Jesus, God dwelled among His creation and endured the cross that no human could bear but Him. Jesus' assignment of the cross took away from us the penalty of sin.

There is more to God than the book of Revelation, and we have yet to see and witness His sovereignty and majesty revealed.

Revelation 1:4 declares:

> *"Him who is and who was and who is to come..."*
>
> — REVELATION 1:4

> *"For those whom He foreknew He also predestined to be conformed to the image of His Son, in order that He might be the firstborn among many brothers. And those whom He predestined He also called, and those whom He called He also justified, and those whom He justified He also glorified."*
>
> — ROMANS 8:29–30

> *"For He chose us in Him before the foundation of the world, that we should be holy and blameless before Him in love. He predestined us to be adopted as His sons through Jesus Christ, according to the good pleasure of His will."*
>
> — EPHESIANS 1:4–5

It is God's will and purpose for us to walk in His predestined plan. We still have our own free will, so we have to make a decision to allow the Holy Spirit to help us walk out what God has planned—because He called us, justified us, and glorified us.

We cannot be holy and blameless before Him in love without Him, which is why we need His Spirit. It is through the person of the Holy Spirit that we are adopted into the family of God through Jesus Christ, and this is good, pleasurable, and in accordance with His will.

Therefore, we are:

- *Called*: to give a specified name; to wake up
- *Justified*: declared or made righteous in the sight of God
- *Glorified*: something ordinary or unacceptable made to appear special; elevated; made glorious

If we look at Romans 8:29–30, we see that God predestined us to be the firstborn—but not only that—He predestined us to be conformed to the image of His Son. So, we were born into the earth before Jesus was, yet made before He was born through the Virgin Mary.

This speaks to the immense value we bring to the earth and how special we are to God. It is through the Word of God that we receive definition. It gives us meaning in life. It explains who we are to God and what our true identity is. Many in the world walk in falsehood simply because they don't know the Word of God that has already been spoken over their lives.

So, if you are reading this, I want you to grasp the fact that you're not just a mere human being. You are a great example of perfection—because God formed you. When you see flaws in yourself, shift your thinking and understand that God made you good. It doesn't matter what anyone or anything says about it—not even your own self.

The more you read the Word, the more you encounter the presence of God. The more you pursue Him in your daily walk, the more you begin to identify with who you really are in Him.

> *"For you have died, and your life has been hidden with Christ in God."*
>
> — COLOSSIANS 3:3

God made it easy for us. We look at it as hard because it's a war—not just any war, but a spiritual war that's trying to fight and distract you from seeing how victorious you are.

We are called. We are awakened spiritually out of our slumber. Then we are justified—we are declared righteous. It is nothing we worked for. It is nothing we did that was so special to deserve it. This is what God did because we are His creation, and we were ordained to do a work in the earth.

And then—He glorified us. He made us a little lower than the angels, and we are gods in the earth. So you have God, then the angels, then man. Do you see the order? Are you beginning to understand who you are now? Is your confidence being built up in Christ Jesus?

I pray that as you read this, the Holy Spirit is revealing to you who you've been all along. You've doubted it. You've fought it. But now you see that the devil—the enemy of your soul—and even your own thoughts shaped by trauma have clouded your identity in Christ Jesus.

> *"For thou hast made him a little lower than the angels, and hast crowned him with glory and honour."*
>
> — PSALM 8:5

> *"Thou madest him a little lower than the angels; thou crownedst him with glory and honour, and didst set him over the works of thy hands: Thou hast put all things in subjection under his feet..."*
>
> — HEBREWS 2:7-9

> *"I said, You are gods, and all of you are children of the Most High."*
>
> — PSALM 82:6

Jesus cites Psalm 82:6 in John 10 during a confrontation with the Jews:

> *"Is it not written in your Law, I have said you are gods? If he called them 'gods,' to whom the word of God came—and Scripture cannot be set aside—what about the one whom the Father set apart as His very own and sent into the world?*
>
> *Why then do you accuse me of blasphemy because I said, I am*

THE HOLY SPIRIT EXPLAINED

God's Son? Believe the works, that you may know and understand that the Father is in me, and I in the Father."

— JOHN 10:34–38

They saw the works Jesus did, yet they denied who He was. He didn't just do works for the Father—He was the Father in the earth. He and the Father were one.

As much as we desire to be accepted—especially by those we love—this shows us something vital: the writing may be on the wall, but unless they walk in the Spirit, people may never see who you really are. Their spirit may not be mature enough to accept the God in you.

But this didn't stop Jesus. They tried to stone Him, yet He continued to do the work of the Father.

Let that be your example.

The Holy Spirit wants you to know—you have to go anyway. You may be rejected, scorned, and ridiculed for representing God in the earth. But be determined not to stop until you are finished.

We are in the Era of Man, which is a period of time marked by significant events, changes, or developments with lasting impact. The Era of Man is both the first and the last—it is the only era that sets the precedent for creation.

When man arrived, the foundation was set. We can also identify this as the Church Age. Had man been created before everything else, he would not have had purpose. He was created to do and to be—to facilitate and manage.

God is a foundational God. He goes ahead of time, prepares, and completes what we are called to walk into. There are a plethora of events and occurrences of God's glory that will happen because we were birthed in the Era of Man.

CHAPTER 2
GOD'S CREATION & FORMATION

In the Hebrew text, "heavenly beings" is Elohim, a common name for God. What does this say about us and who we are in the earth?

> "What is man that you are mindful of him, and the son of man that you care for him? Yet you have made him a little lower than the heavenly beings and crowned him with glory and honor."
>
> — PSALM 8:4-5

To have God's hand form us by Himself with no other assistance—when we look at the details of our entire being, why God made every part of us, what those particular parts represent, and how they all flow together—man can look at us as a creation of complex people. But God looks at us as perfect. He looks at us and sees Himself. All of us can be found in Him.

You know how, when you have your natural parents, you see traits of the child that resemble the mother, and you see traits of the father.

Then you can go further back through generations and see different traits from both sides—grandparents, great-grandparents, and so on.

We were created in resemblance of God—both in character and in appearance. He used the word *likeness*.

1. Resemblance in form; similitude.
2. Resemblance; form; external appearance.
3. One that resembles another; a copy; a counterpart.

> *"Then God said, "Let Us make man in Our image, according to Our likeness; let them have dominion over the fish of the sea, over the birds of the air, and over the cattle, over all the earth and over every creeping thing that creeps on the earth." So God created mankind in His own image; in the image of God He created them; male and female He created them."*
>
> — GENESIS 1:26–27

God created mankind in His likeness and image—born male and female. Later, in Chapter 2, it states that man was made first and the rib was taken out of man to make woman.

> *"Then the Lord God formed a man from the dust of the ground and breathed into his nostrils the breath of life, and the man became a living being."*
>
> — GENESIS 2:7

What is the difference between being created and being formed? Let's explore both, together.

UNDERSTANDING "CREATION"

To *create* means to bring something into existence. It was an announcement of what was to come. This is how we create—we speak it. God said, "Let Us make man in Our likeness and image." He made man with a purpose. Right after the announcement came the purpose.

Isn't this how we all develop things in our lives? It is created in our minds, and it is formed through our actions. So, our mind is the place where we envision what God has formed us to do, and we start doing it through the leading of the Holy Spirit by specific instructions.

> *"Let them have dominion over the fish of the sea, over the birds of the air, and over the cattle, over all the earth and over every creeping thing that creeps on the earth."*
>
> — GENESIS 1:26

We were created for purposes—to do something. And the entire first chapter of Genesis was the ground being set for God's creation to manage what He created. So, He put it all in place first. Our purpose was in place before we came along, and then God shared our purpose. He had in mind what He wanted man to do before He gave man the charge.

The Triune God had a major part to play in our creation. You have *God the Father, God the Son,* and *God the Holy Spirit*. So, how do all three relate to us being formed in His likeness?

1. God the Father:

The attributes of our natural father are to provide, to protect, to cover, to teach, to groom, to make sure you grow, and to help you excel to your full potential. God's nature transcends human comprehension—He is wholly unique, incomparable, and impossible to fully describe with mere words. Nonetheless, through Scripture, He reveals certain attributes that help us understand Him.

These are divided into:

- *Incommunicable attributes:* qualities unique to God alone (such as omnipotence, omniscience, etc.)

- *Communicable attributes:* qualities shared with humans, though only God possesses them perfectly (like love, wisdom, mercy).

2. God the Son:

Then we have Jesus Christ, the Son of God, who is our Mediator. Jesus went the length to sacrifice His life in obedience to His Father, to make sure He bridged the gap and brought us into eternal life back to our Father.

His life here on earth resembled our Father, and therefore we were able to see and feel the Father's love through His Son. His Son gave us the example of how to do the same thing—to feel the Father's love, to experience the Father's love, and to allow others to experience it through us.

3. God the Holy Spirit

We have the person of the Holy Spirit, who is our inward help given by God, who is God and lives inside of us to make sure we live an effective life in obedience to every Word of God.

The whole idea is that the Holy Spirit can be our voice, our eyes, and our ears. We have this body totally yielded to God, but what God wants to release and do—we are empowered to do that through Himself, through the Spirit of God, through the Holy Spirit.

4. Triune God (Trinity)

There is one God who exists eternally as three distinct but equal

Persons: the Father, the Son, and the Holy Spirit. Scripture provides evidence of this unity and distinction, such as:

> *"The grace of the Lord Jesus Christ, the love of God, and the fellowship of the Holy Spirit be with you all."*
>
> — 2 CORINTHIANS 13:14

> *"Therefore go and make disciples of all nations, baptizing them in the name of the Father and of the Son and of the Holy Spirit."*
>
> — MATTHEW 28:19

Together, these passages show that while the Father, Son, and Spirit carry out different roles, they share the same divine nature and work in perfect harmony.

5. The Father and the Son

> *"'Do not let your hearts be troubled. You believe in God; believe in Me as well. In My Father's house are many rooms. If it were not so, would I have told you that I am going there to prepare a place for you? And if I go and prepare a place for you, I will come back and welcome you into My presence, so that you also may be where I am. You know the way to the place where I am going.'*
> *'Lord,' said Thomas, 'we do not know where You are going, so how can we know the way?'*
> *Jesus answered, 'I am the way and the truth and the life. No one comes to the Father except through Me. If you had known Me, you would know My Father as well. From now on you do know Him and have seen Him.'*
> *Philip said to Him, 'Lord, show us the Father, and that will be enough for us.'*

> *Jesus replied, 'Philip, I have been with you all this time, and still you do not know Me? Anyone who has seen Me has seen the Father. How can you say, 'Show us the Father'? Do you not believe that I am in the Father and the Father is in Me? The words I say to you, I do not speak on My own. Instead, it is the Father dwelling in Me, performing His works. Believe Me that I am in the Father and the Father is in Me—or at least believe on account of the works themselves. Truly, truly, I tell you, whoever believes in Me will also do the works that I am doing. He will do even greater things than these, because I am going to the Father. And I will do whatever you ask in My name, so that the Father may be glorified in the Son. If you ask Me for anything in My name, I will do it.'"*
>
> — JOHN 14:1–14

> *"If you love Me, you will keep My commandments. And I will ask the Father, and He will give you another Advocate to be with you forever—the Spirit of truth. The world cannot receive Him, because it neither sees Him nor knows Him. But you do know Him, for He abides with you and will be in you. I will not leave you as orphans; I will come to you. In a little while the world will see Me no more, but you will see Me. Because I live, you also will live. On that day you will know that I am in My Father, and you are in Me, and I am in you."*
>
> — JOHN 14:15-21

It was a progression even in the creative aspect. God made man first, then gave him dominion:

> *"...let them have dominion over the fish of the sea, over the*

> *birds of the air, and over the cattle, over all the earth and over every creeping thing that creeps on the earth."*
>
> — GENESIS 1:26-28

The Word activates. He made man with dominion, but announced it in the earth, and all creation responded. All creation now knows that it has to be subject to the authority of man's voice, given by God.

God announced man, made man, created and formed man. He then brought the distinction between the two—male and female. He made it very clear that, yes, it was mankind, but it was two types: In the image of God, He created "them" (Genesis 1:27).

He already had in mind that when He created man, woman was already formulated. He took her from him to connect them formally. Prior to bringing her out of him, there was the establishing of foundation first—God's divine order.

Then He brought her into the picture. So God, in the natural as well, establishes the man and gets the man in order so that when the woman comes, he has the foundation of his life established by God already.

When we read the Bible, we always get revelation of the order of God and how He puts things in place. This is also the example—the prototype—of marriage. The man is considered the head of the household, and he is to lead the home as Christ is leading him.

> *"But I want you to understand that the head of every man is Christ, the head of a wife is her husband, and the head of Christ is God."*
>
> — 1 CORINTHIANS 11:3

> *"For the husband is the head of the wife even as Christ is the head of the church, His body, and is Himself its Savior."*
>
> — EPHESIANS 5:23

CRYSTAL LOVE

> *"Then the Lord God said, "It is not good that the man should be alone; I will make him a helper fit for him."*
>
> — GENESIS 2:18

> *"Likewise, husbands, live with your wives in an understanding way, showing honor to the woman as the weaker vessel, since they are heirs with you of the grace of life, so that your prayers may not be hindered."*
>
> — 1 PETER 3:7

Other translations of 1 Peter 3:7 render the phrase as "weaker partner" (NIV, CSB), "someone weaker" (NASB), or "weaker than you are" (NLT). There are many speculations about what Paul was referring to as the "weaker vessel."

The most common proposal is physical weakness. Other suggestions include that women are less in control of their emotions, or that women are more easily deceived (based on 1 Timothy 2:14). However, the Bible as a whole does not specifically say that women are weaker than men.

The consequence of a husband not honoring his wife is hindered prayer—something every believing husband should attempt to avoid. Whatever "weaker vessel" means, the application is that husbands are to understand, honor, and value their wives.

In context, "weaker vessel" likely carries the meaning of "worth protecting" and "something to cherish" far more than it is intended to identify specific weaknesses or in any way diminish the strength and value of wives. A husband must love his wife as Christ loved the church and gave His life for it.

So the establishment of man is very important to the woman, so that she can come on board to help and carry out the assignment of God together. God blessed them because they were one.

The Bride of Christ is made up of many people, while the Bridegroom is Christ—one Person of the Godhead, and at the same time all three. This is why it is so important to come together, to join together, because we help each other prepare.

We're getting dressed. We're cleaning up. We're planning. He's coming to get His blameless, beautiful Bride, and we all have to make sure that we are ready.

> *"Then God blessed them."*
>
> — GENESIS 1:28

We were on the mind of God. We were spoken. We were created with a purpose—for a purpose—and then God gave us our purpose. He gave us something to do, and then He blessed (to make holy; consecrated) us.

Now, if we were created in the likeness and image of God, and He created us with His purpose, why does He have to turn around and bless us? Shouldn't we already be blessed?

Though we were created in His likeness and His image, we were still apart from Him. He anointed them to carry out the assignment. Again, this is the announcement—the establishment—in the earth.

This is the third time I am coming to you. In the mouth of two or three witnesses shall every word be established.

Then He added to the list of fulfillment:

> *"And God said to them, 'Be fruitful and multiply; fill the earth and subdue it; have dominion over the fish of the sea, over the birds of the air, and over every living thing that moves on the earth.'"*
>
> — 2 CORINTHIANS 13:1–4

He repeated the same thing in another verse:

> *"Let them have dominion over the fish of the sea, over the*

birds of the air, and over the cattle, over all the earth and over every creeping thing that creeps on the earth."

— GENESIS 1:26

The only part missing from the first command is the cattle and living things. What was added in the latter one was every creeping thing.

ALL LIVING THINGS

All living things share life processes such as growth and reproduction. All living things move in some way. This may be obvious—such as animals that are able to walk—or less obvious, such as plants that have parts that move to track the movement of the sun. *Respiration* is a chemical reaction that happens within cells to release energy from food.

- *All living things* have the ability to detect changes in the surrounding environment.

- *All living things* grow.

- *All living things* reproduce and pass genetic information on to their offspring.

- *All living things* get rid of waste.

- *All living things* take in and use nutrients, though this occurs in very different ways depending on the kind of living thing.

Examples include birds, insects, animals, trees, and human beings—all of which share the same characteristic features: eating, breathing, reproduction, growth, and development.

God gave man dominion—over man, over ourselves—and told us:

> "Be fruitful and multiply; fill the earth and subdue (to overcome or bring under control) it."
>
> — GENESIS 1:28

We were blessed, created, and purposed to produce, grow, live, expand—given power, authority, and blessing to keep things in order. The attributes of God inside of us help sustain us and enable us to help each other manage all that God has given us.

And then He yielded even more. He gave us food to sustain us. He provides for us, and everything we needed was in the garden, in the presence of God.

> "And God said, "See, I have given you every herb that yields seed which is on the face of all the earth, and every tree whose fruit yields seed; to you it shall be for food. Also, to every beast of the earth, to every bird of the air, and to everything that creeps on the earth, in which there is life, I have given every green herb for food"; and it was so. Then God saw everything that He had made, and indeed it was very good. So the evening and the morning were the sixth day."
>
> — GENESIS 1:29–31

THE CREATION VS. THE FORMATION

To *create* means to bring something into existence— to lay the foundation. That means it's heard; the foundation is set. To *form* refers to the visible shape or configuration of something— to bring together parts or combine to create something. The *form* is the definition—the details that bring the vision to light.

We were created in His likeness and image in the spirit. Then, He formed us in the natural—from the dust of the earth—and breathed into man, and he became a living soul. This is the work of the Triune God and the unfolding of His plan.

CHAPTER 3
EMPOWERED TO TAKE DOMINION

The Word of God—the fulfillment of God—was spirit. Then the Word became flesh through His Son Jesus when He came to do the work of His Father. He came as the Son, left us the example of how we should carry on, and gave us help to live within us.

> *"In the beginning was the Word, and the Word was with God, and the Word was God. He was with God in the beginning."*
>
> — JOHN 1:1–2

The Word is spirit. We are a living word made manifest in flesh and empowered to take dominion in the earth by the Spirit of God—the Holy Spirit.

The Holy Spirit is the flow and the cause of movement to bring the vision to life—the vision of man. One of the main symbols of the Holy Spirit throughout Scripture is *water*.

Water does not stay still. Water flows and moves—through streams to oceans, rivers, muddy places, stony places, sandy places, and even dry places. Water doesn't stop flowing. It can dry up, but the only way that water can dry up is if the flow stops. The only way we can stop the flow of the Holy Spirit in our lives is if we step out of the flow—if we stop listening to the Holy Spirit and His instructions.

When God breathed the breath of life into man, that was the Holy Spirit—that was the flow. Everything in the body was formed, but the breath caused it to come to life and to move in rhythm with God.

If we stay in the flow of God—in the wind of God—everything in our life will always produce and move forward. There will never be stagnation in our lives if we allow the Holy Spirit to flow.

There will be times when it doesn't seem like things are happening, but they are. There will be times where it may seem like life is at a standstill, but that's not the truth. God has a set time and season for things to manifest in the earth. Just because we don't see movement here doesn't mean that things are not moving. Things are always moving in the Spirit.

Man became a living soul—both in the natural and in the spirit. In both realms. We were created in the spirit realm, formed into the earth realm, and blessed—equipped to live in both realms through the Holy Spirit.

WE HAVE DOMINION & AUTHORITY

Psalm 8:6 continues,

> *"You have given him dominion over the works of your hands;*
> *you have put all things under his feet."*
>
> — PSALM 8:6

The psalmist understood from Genesis 1:26–28 that God gave mankind the authority to rule over the created world. We have authority over the world that was already put together. God is the author and finisher of our faith. He set the stage and wanted mankind to maintain it. God is confident about His creation because He declared that we were good.

The works of your hands is God hands. He put all things under our feet meaning we have power over it. *This means all things!*

> *"What is man that You are mindful of him, And the son of*
> *man that You visit him? For You have made him a little*
> *lower than the angels. And You have crowned him with*
> *glory and honor. You have made him to have dominion*
> *over the works of Your hands; You have put*
> *all things under his feet."*
>
> — PSALM 8:4-6

When the Word says that God is mindful, it means that He has taken under consideration what He has invested in man, which is Himself.

The title "son of man" reminds us that humanity existed in the earth-man before Jesus came in the flesh, even though Jesus Himself existed long before us. When we look at Scripture, we see many reasons for the order in which God speaks and acts—why He says what He says and how He says it. Jesus was attended to and appointed by God to complete His assignment on the Earth. He came to die once and for all as the ultimate sacrifice for our sins. While we live on this earth, we are also dying daily, crucifying our flesh so that our spirit-man can have full reign in our lives.

The Hebrew word for "visit" is *paqad*, which means "to attend to, muster, or appoint." The title "son of man" can refer to Adam as the head of humanity. Created with a human body and given authority, Adam was made "a little lower" than the angels, yet he was crowned with glory and honor because he was made in the image of God.

In Hebrews 2:6–8, the writer quotes Psalm 8:5 and explains that all creation was placed in subjection to the Son of Man:

> *"In putting everything in subjection to him, he left nothing outside his control."*
>
> — HEBREWS 2:8

The author of Hebrews then identifies the "son of man" as Jesus Christ:

> *"But we see him who for a little while was made lower than the angels, namely Jesus, crowned with glory and honor because of the suffering of death, so that by the grace of God he might taste death for everyone."*
>
> — HEBREWS 2:9

We are compared to Jesus because we follow a similar pattern: we come from God, we enter the earth, and just as Jesus returned to God, we will return, as well. When the earth is destroyed, the physical body—the old man, the dust—returns to the ground, and everything produced by the flesh is burned up once and for all.

> *"He is the radiance of the glory of God and the exact imprint of His nature, and He upholds the universe by the word of His power. After making purification for sins, He sat down at the right hand of the Majesty on high."*
>
> — HEBREWS 1:3

THE NEW ADAM

Applying Psalm 8:5 to Jesus Christ, the writer of Hebrews uses the title "son of man" to emphasize the humanity of Christ, His connection to the first Adam, and His place as the greatest example of man. Jesus Christ is truly the Second Adam, the new Adam, who came to deal directly with what the first Adam brought upon mankind and could never defeat—namely, death.

> *"And so it is written, 'The first man Adam became a living being.' The last Adam became a life-giving spirit."*
>
> — 1 CORINTHIANS 15:45

Nothing is outside of our control when it pertains to what God has given us dominion over! It is now the sixth hour. This is the hour to awaken, but the death process must take place first. When you awaken, the death sentence is pronounced on anything that rocked your purpose to sleep.

> *"It was now about the sixth hour (noon), and darkness came over the whole land until the ninth hour (3:00 p.m.), because the sun was obscured; and the veil of the temple was torn in two."*
>
> — LUKE 23:44–46

Scripture tells us it was noon, yet darkness fell—an hour when darkness was not expected. Darkness came just before Jesus released His spirit to God the Father. The absence of the sun foreshadowed the departure of the Son from the physical earth and revealed what life is like without the Son of God.

This mirrors our own lives. Right before a blessing arrives, chaos often seems to break loose. It can look as if everything is falling apart, but God is allowing things to dissolve so that the new can come. Leaving one place and entering another rarely feels smooth. Darkness is not always a sign of chaos—it can be a time of uncertainty when it feels as if God is silent. Yet after God gives us a word and we begin to walk in it, there may come a moment when we ask, "Lord, what is next? What do I do now?" God's answer is: Stay with what I gave you. If He is not giving new instruction, continue in His last direction. Do not create something on your own. Wait for the next instruction. It will come.

The next part of the passage says the veil was torn from top to bottom, leading into the Holy of Holies. This sacred place was covered by a veil, and no one was allowed to enter except the High Priest, and only once a year on Yom Kippur to offer sacrifice and incense. When darkness fell, the separation was broken, and the dwelling place of the God of Israel became open and accessible to all. Through the sacrifice of the Lamb of God, the final offering was given, granting us direct access to God.

I declare that every area of your life lacking the light of God will be illuminated and revealed. You will walk in the light and bring every weakness, flaw, and insecurity into the presence of God—into the Holy of Holies. In that place there is no condemnation or flaw; there is only His glory. When you stand there, you see no sin—you see glory. Let us aim to live there.

Looking at the pattern of the Tabernacle of Moses, those who came to sacrifice brought slaughtered animals. Consider the "slaughtered" places in your life: the shattered perception of yourself, the visions that did not come to pass, the marriage that ended in divorce, the friendships that ended in betrayal, the clouded mind that kept you from seeing what God placed before you. These are messy, bloody places, yet there is beauty there. After the animals were slaughtered, the priests went to the bronze laver to wash. The laver functioned like a mirror. As you read this book, allow God to wash you with His Word so you can see your true identity and move into the Holy Place, where the table of showbread and the candlestick are located.

Let's dive deeper.

The Ark of the Covenant—also called the Ark of the Testimony or the Ark of God—is considered the most sacred relic of the Israelites. It is described as a wooden chest covered in pure gold, with an ornate lid called the mercy seat. According to *Exodus*, the Ark contained the two stone tablets of the Ten Commandments, Aaron's rod, and a pot of manna. One year after the Israelites' exodus from Egypt, the Ark was created according to the pattern God gave Moses at Mount Sinai. During their forty years in the desert, the Ark was carried with them and placed within a separate room in the sacred tent called the Tabernacle.

On Mount Sinai, Moses received not only the Ten Commandments but also detailed instructions for building a meeting place for God and His people. The Tabernacle was a place of worship with specific protocols and procedures that allowed God's people to dwell with Him as He requested.

> *"Let them make Me a sanctuary, that I may dwell among them."*
>
> — EXODUS 25:8

From the fall in Genesis until the construction of the Tabernacle, Scripture records people occasionally walking with God but not dwelling with Him. Within the framework of this sanctuary, God draws His people closer through an intricate sacrificial system. This arrangement speaks powerfully to us today about the depth of our salvation and the indescribable gift God has provided.

CHAPTER 4
GOD USES SYSTEMS

What are systems? A system is a command joined with structure. Your life is a command from God, joined with His instructions, forming patterns that shape your development and bring forth maturity in every season. You have developed a rhythm that governs your relationship with God.

Let's break down the word...

- *Sys* — a basic command joined together
- *Tem* — system, structure, or a specific part of something

> "And we know that all things work together for good to them that love God, to them who are the called according to His purpose."
>
> — ROMANS 8:28

The thing about development is this: you cannot grow when your system is broken. Systems determine how things operate. Computers, for example, have operating systems. When something malfunctions—your printer, your software—the first step in troubleshooting is identifying the system you're using. The same is true spiritually. Your spiritual operating system reveals the recurring issues in your life.

If you take time to assess your life, ask God to show you your patterns.

There are four things that determine how your life flows:

1. Operating systems
2. Patterns
3. Development
4. Maturity

These four areas will never fully align—nor be revealed—without the Holy Spirit and revelation. Many people flow in their spiritual gifts, which God gives without repentance, but gifting alone does not equal maturity.

> *"For the gifts and calling of God are without repentance."*
>
> — ROMANS 11:29

You do not have to be flawless to flow in a gift. Never mistake someone's (or your own) ability to operate in a spiritual gift as evidence of full maturity or effectiveness in your calling. Revelation does not equal spirituality. Even Solomon—the wisest man to ever live—fell because of disobedience.

> *"For rebellion is as the sin of witchcraft, and stubbornness is as iniquity and idolatry. Because thou hast rejected the word of the Lord, he hath also rejected thee from being king."*
>
> — 1 SAMUEL 15:23

When we reject God's instruction or fail to obey His voice, we step into rebellion.

THE HOLY SPIRIT EXPLAINED

WHAT SYSTEM IS GOVERNING YOUR MIND?

We often create our own operating systems based on experiences, learned behaviors, and spiritual patterns.

Development asks: "What is shaping you?" Whatever feeds you—whatever you listen to, watch, focus on, or remain connected to—develops you. Development can lead to expansion and maturity, or it can simply form habits that have nothing to do with God. It all depends on your focus. What you focus on will rule your life. That is your operating system.

When you rely only on your own system, you are forced to troubleshoot every issue yourself. But when you walk in the Spirit—according to God's order and His system—He handles the troubleshooting. He empowers you so that you will not fulfill the lust of the flesh. His system produces fruit—the fruit of the Spirit, not frustration.

A kingdom is a territory ruled by a king or queen. The earth is our territory as kings and priests. We are reclaiming both the spiritual kingdom, where God governs through the Gospel and the Church, and the earthly realm, where He governs through law and civil authority. Hierarchy exists because someone must rule.

The problem with the world today is that its systems are not influenced by the Spirit of God. This is why the world keeps malfunctioning—it produces fruit, but not fruit from God's kingdom.

In the Kingdom of God, there is only one operating system: the Holy Spirit, maturing us through the Word of God.

> Do you see any progress? If not, why?
> Who are you listening to?
> Who are you connected to?
> What is distracting you?
> Are you mature enough to handle the truth about your life?

You have been trying to build with broken pieces. You have been picking up shattered glass—trying to see yourself through a broken mirror. God says, "Let Me clean that up for you. That mirror broke a long time ago. Stop picking up the old you—the broken you. There's a new you that you've never seen before."

When Jesus rose from the grave, they did not recognize Him. You are about to rise from a dead place. They pronounced you dead, but they never checked for a pulse. You are about to be resurrected, and people will not recognize who you are. God will get the glory, because the dead parts of you will no longer define you.

New systems!
Patterns changed!
Paths renewed!
Development restored!
Maturity manifested!

What patterns are you repeating that are actually creating change? God is bringing definition to your purpose—your assignment—your destiny. Everything you do, everyone you spend time with, everything you give attention to—all these things shape you.

Do you value your life enough to make serious, even abrupt, changes?

No more procrastination.

No more demonic cycles.

You cannot allow anyone to speak or impart something into your life that God did not ordain. What God placed inside you from the foundation of the world must be released.

You must *go* and *grow!*

Many things contribute to delays, but fear is the root that clusters with others. Fear grips you so you do not move in God's timing.

THE CANDLESTICK: A PICTURE OF THE HOLY SPIRIT

Israel was commanded to bring offerings and build the Tabernacle: the Ark of the Testimony (with the mercy seat and cherubim), the

THE HOLY SPIRIT EXPLAINED

table for the showbread, and the candlestick—all made according to the pattern God showed Moses on the mountain.

Let us focus on the candlestick, which represents the work of the Holy Spirit.

> *And thou shalt make a candlestick of pure gold: of beaten work shall the candlestick be made: his shaft, and his branches, his bowls, his knops, and his flowers, shall be of the same.*
> *And six branches shall come out of the sides of it; three branches of the candlestick out of the one side, and three branches of the candlestick out of the other side: three bowls made like unto almonds, with a knop and a flower in one branch; and three bowls made like almonds in the other branch, with a knop and a flower: so in the six branches that come out of the candlestick.*
> *And in the candlestick shall be four bowls made like unto almonds, with their knops and their flowers. And there shall be a knop under two branches of the same, a knop under two branches of the same, and a knop under two branches of the same, according to the six branches that proceed out of the candlestick. Their knops and their branches shall be of the same: all of it shall be one beaten work of pure gold.*
> *And thou shalt make the seven lamps thereof: and they shall light the lamps thereof, that they may give light over against it. And the tongs thereof, and the snuff dishes thereof, shall be of pure gold. Of a talent of pure gold shall he make it, with all these vessels.*
> *And look that thou make them after their pattern, which was showed thee in the mount."*
>
> — EXODUS 25:31-40

Like the mercy seat, the candlestick was made entirely of pure gold. Unlike many parts of the Tabernacle constructed from shittim wood, every detail of the candlestick was pure gold.

> *These tests have come to prove your faith and to show that it is good. Gold, which can be destroyed, is tested by fire.*
>
> — 1 PETER 1:7 (NIV)

> *Your faith is worth much more than gold and it must be tested, also. Then, your faith will bring thanks and shining-greatness and honor to Jesus Christ when He comes again.*
>
> — 1 PETER 1:7 (NLV)

These trials will show that your faith is genuine. It is being tested as fire tests and purifies gold—though your faith is far more precious than mere gold. So when your faith remains strong through many trials, it will bring you much praise and glory and honor on the day when Jesus Christ is revealed to the whole world.

This passage of Scripture, shown here in two different translations, teaches us that beyond the purification of the gold used for the candlestick, we—God's creation and His children—are also refined through the tests we endure. These tests reveal where our faith truly is. They show whether we believe God and remind us that the measure of faith He has given us is all we need. Gold, as described in Scripture, can be destroyed and is proven by fire, but what God has placed inside of us is stronger than gold.

Trials benefit us because they show us what we have and what we need to sharpen. They highlight impurities—not for condemnation, but so we can allow God to deliver us from those things and free us to walk in the fullness of God. The consuming fire of God brings both death and life: death to the things that must be stripped away, and life to the areas that need to be awakened, birthed, and rebirthed.

THE OIL AND THE LIGHT

In Exodus 27:20, we learn that the light was fed by "pure oil olive beaten for the light, to cause the lamp to burn always." Oil in Scripture is consistently a symbol of the Holy Spirit. But in order for oil to be produced, the olives must be crushed. The crushing removes bitterness. In the same manner, Jesus was crushed under the burden and weight of our sins and under the judgment of a holy God. The apostle writes of believers, "Ye have an unction from the Holy One" (1 John 2:20), and also speaks of our having been "anointed" (2 Corinthians 1:21).

When we combine these three elements in their symbolic meaning —the number seven, the gold, and the oil—the significance of the candlestick becomes clear: it represents divine light in its perfection through the power of the Spirit. It is God giving the light of the Holy Spirit, displayed in its sevenfold perfection. Addressing the church in Sardis, the Lord speaks of having "the seven Spirits of God" (Revelation 3:1), that is, the Spirit in His perfection (as indicated by the number seven) and power. We also read of "seven lamps of fire burning before the throne, which are the seven Spirits of God" (Revelation 4:5).

What, then, was the purpose of the candlestick? It appears to have been twofold:

1. First, it was set in the holy place "over against the table" (Exodus 25:27; 26:35; 40:24).

Positioned opposite the table of showbread, it cast its light upon it. This placement suggests intention. The table of showbread symbolizes, as explained in the previous chapter, the manifestation of God in man (Christ) in the perfection of divine government. The twelve loaves represent Israel, and in principle, believers of this dispensation, standing in association with Christ before God.

Thus, the candlestick's light shining upon the table signifies the Holy Spirit bearing testimony to the future display of Christ's perfect administration when He takes His power and reigns from the river to the ends of the earth. It also testifies to Israel's—and the believer's—true place in connection with Christ before God. Though these truths may be obscured or forgotten on earth, in the holy place, before the eye of God, they are fully displayed in the perfect light of the Spirit.

2. *Second*, the candlestick's light illuminated itself.

> "And the Lord spake unto Moses, saying, Speak unto Aaron, and say unto him, When thou lightest the lamps, the seven lamps shall give light over against the candlestick. And Aaron did so; he lighted the lamps thereof over against the candlestick, as the Lord commanded Moses."
>
> — NUMBERS 8:1–3

This shows that the light of the Holy Spirit reveals and glorifies the vessel through which it shines. A perfect illustration of this is seen in the transfiguration of our blessed Lord: "His face did shine as the sun, and His raiment was white as the light" (Matthew 17:2). This radiance marked His entire earthly pathway for those whose eyes were opened (John 1:4; 2:11), but on the mount, His beauty was openly and unmistakably displayed.

JESUS OUR APOSTLE AND HIGH PRIEST

> *Wherefore, holy brethren, partakers of the heavenly calling, consider the Apostle and High Priest of our profession [or confession], Christ Jesus.*
>
> — HEBREWS 3:1

There is a mystery to the apostleship and priesthood of Jesus. An apostle means "sent one," so Jesus was sent from God to accomplish a specific work on our behalf. He has been sent to serve as our High Priest. A high priest is one who is authorized to administer, execute, implement, and carry into effect. Jesus is fully authorized to administer, execute, and carry out actions on your behalf.

According to Hebrews 3:1, Jesus is the High Priest of our confession. He has been sent to put into effect, to execute, and to carry out the words we speak. Therefore, the words we declare should be the Word of the Lord:

> *"It shall come to pass That before they call, I will answer; And while they are still speaking, I will hear."*
>
> — ISAIAH 65:24

The word *shema* in Hebrew means "to hear, to pay attention, and to respond." God hears us—and requires us to hear Him with the same attentiveness. It is call and response. This is why so many of the cries for help in the book of Psalms begin with a call that God listen.

> *"Hear my voice when I call, Lord; be merciful to me and answer me."*
>
> — PSALM 27:7

In Exodus 24:7, the people say,

> *"All that the LORD has spoken we will do, and we will be obedient (shema)!"*
>
> — EXODUS 24:7

The word shema is also the name of the "pledge of allegiance" that Jesus and other observant Jews say every morning and evening. The first line of the pledge is "Hear (Shema), O Israel! The LORD is our

God, the LORD alone." God listens, He hears us, and He responds; He desires us to do the same thing.

IT IS YOUR TIME TO RISE

For the believers of Christ: it is our time to soar and to walk in the authority God has purposed for us. What are you waiting for? It is not too late—start now. Surrender your will and let God's will take over your life. Your life in the Lord's hands is in good care. You will soar in this era.

The sixth hour is the hour of reckoning—the moment of calculation and gathering. God is bringing together what belongs to you in order to lead you into what He promised. Let this era shine because you showed up. You have access. The unveiled you will be revealed to the world.

On the last day of creation, when man was made, God introduced creation to its leader—its first leader. Why did God rest on the seventh day, and what did that rest symbolize? He knew that what He made was good and fully sufficient to leave a lasting impression on the earth. His work was done.

Rest means it is finished.

I can rest, hope, and trust in God because I am walking out the finished work, so I will complete it. No matter what fallen state you have found yourself in, remember this: you are no longer under the curse but under the blood. Let your impartation—imputed to you by the blood—multiply and resound in the earth.

It is your time to make history.

CHAPTER 5
HOW IT ALL BEGAN

God knew from the very beginning that we could not walk through this life on our own. That is why He invites us into relationship with Him—not just any relationship, but a deeply intimate one. He desires closeness because He knows we need His help. We cannot live out the fullness of God's purpose without Him at the center. There is simply no way to accomplish it apart from Him. Without His insight, guidance, and wisdom, our efforts will always fall short. So if you have not yet become closely acquainted with the Holy Spirit, now is the time to begin that journey.

We first encounter the Spirit of God in Genesis 1:2:

> "The earth was without form and void, and darkness was over the face of the deep. And the Spirit of God was hovering over the face of the waters."
>
> — GENESIS 1:2

This verse does more than describe God's presence; it introduces us to the person of the Holy Spirit, distinct yet fully God. Here we begin to see the mystery of the Trinity unfold—the Godhead, three in one.

While Scripture consistently affirms that there is only one God, it also reveals His triune nature:

> "Hear, O Israel: The Lord our God, the Lord is one."
>
> — DEUTERONOMY 6:4

> "...there is no other God but one."
>
> — 1 CORINTHIANS 8:4

> "Now a mediator is not for one party only; but God is one."
>
> — GALATIANS 3:20

> "For there is one God and one mediator between God and mankind, the man Christ Jesus."
>
> — 1 TIMOTHY 2:5

The Godhead—Father, Son, and Holy Spirit—is a divine unity. *1 Timothy* reminds us that God does not need a mediator because there is no lack in Him. Yet Christ, fully God and fully man, became our Mediator. He came in the flesh to be the sacrifice and in the Spirit to ascend. This dual nature is essential for understanding His role in redemption.

THE ATTRIBUTES OF GOD

The attributes of God describe His nature, personality, and actions.

- Consuming Fire (*Deuteronomy 4:24*)
- Great and Awesome (*Deuteronomy 7:21*)

- Refuge *(Psalm 46:1)*
- Mighty One *(Psalm 50:1)*
- Merciful *(Psalm 116:5)*
- Counselor *(Isaiah 9:6)*
- Salvation *(Isaiah 12:2)*
- Savior *(Luke 1:47)*
- Spirit *(John 4:24)*
- Faithful *(1 Corinthians 1:9)*
- Love *(1 John 4:8)*
- Supplier *(Philippians 4:19)*
- King *(Psalm 47:7)*

Below are ten additional key attributes of God, along with supporting Scriptures.

1. Omnipotence (All-Powerful)

God is all-powerful and has complete control over all things.

- *Psalm 115:3*: "Our God is in heaven; He does whatever pleases Him."

- *Isaiah 46:10*: "My counsel shall stand, and I will accomplish all My purpose."

- *Jeremiah 32:17*: "Ah, Lord God! It is You who have made the heavens and the earth by Your great power and by Your outstretched arm! Nothing is too hard for You."

2. Omniscience (All-Knowing)

God knows all things—past, present, and future.

- *Psalm 139:1–2*: "You have searched me, Lord, and you know me. You know when I sit and when I rise; you perceive my thoughts from afar."

- *Proverbs 15:3*: "The eyes of the Lord are everywhere, keeping watch on the wicked and the good."

- *1 John 3:20*: "For whatever is born of God overcomes the world; and this is the victory that has overcome the world—our faith."

3. Omnipresence (Always Present)

God is present everywhere and is not limited by space or time.

- *Psalm 139:7–12*: "Where can I go from your Spirit? Or where can I flee from your presence? If I say, 'Surely the darkness will hide me and the light become night around me,' even the darkness will not be dark to you; the night will shine like the day, for darkness is as light to you."

- *Jeremiah 23:23–24*: "Am I a God near at hand, says the Lord, and not a God far off? Can a man hide in secret places so that I do not see him? says the Lord. Do I not fill heaven and earth? says the Lord."

- *Acts 7:48–50*: "The Most High does not live in houses made by hands... for he is the Lord our God, who divided the sea and the land, and who made a dry path through the deep sea..."

4. Eternal (Without Beginning or End)

God is eternal and has always existed. He has no beginning and will never end.

- *Psalm 90:2:* "From everlasting to everlasting you are God."

- *Psalm 102:12:* "But you, O Lord, sit enthroned forever; your name endures to all generations."

- *Revelation 1:8:* "I am the Alpha and the Omega, the beginning and the end."

5. Immutable (Unchangeable)

God is unchanging and does not change His nature or character.

- *Hebrews 1:11-12:* "They will perish, but you remain; they will all wear out like a garment. You change them like a cloak, and they will be changed."

- *Malachi 3:6:* "For I the Lord do not change; therefore you, O children of Jacob, are not consumed."

- *James 1:17:* "For it is not because of any works done by us that we made known to you the riches of the glory of this mystery among the Gentiles, which comes from Christ and from the hope that lies hidden within him; and for the mystery is not revealed to those who are in the world but it has now been revealed to us and through the Holy Spirit has been clearly shown to His holy apostles and prophets in the scriptures."

6. Infinite (Limitless)

God is infinite and has no limits or bounds.

- *Psalm 90:2:* "From everlasting to everlasting you are God."

- *Isaiah 40:28:* "Do you not know? Have you not heard? The Lord is the everlasting God, the Creator of the ends of the earth. He will not grow tired or weary, and his understanding no one can fathom."

- *Jeremiah 32:17:* "Ah, Lord God! It is you who have made the heavens and the earth by your great power and by your outstretched arm! Nothing is too hard for you."

7. Just (Fair and Righteous)

God is just and fair in all His actions and judgments.

- *Psalm 97:2:* "Righteousness and justice are the foundation of your throne; love and faithfulness go before you."

- *Isaiah 5:16:* "But the Lord Almighty is exalted by his justice, and the Holy God shows himself holy in his righteousness."

- *Revelation 19:11:* "Then I saw heaven opened, and a white horse was seen coming out. The horse was called Faithful and True, and in righteousness he judges and wages war."

8. Holy (Morally Purer)

God is morally pure and perfect in all His ways.

- *Isaiah 6:3:* "Each of the four living creatures had six wings and was covered with eyes all around and all within. They never rest day or night, saying: 'Holy, holy, holy is the Lord God Almighty, who was, and is, and is to come.'"

- *Revelation 4:8:* "Each of the four living creatures had six wings and was covered with eyes around and within, and day and night they never cease to sing, 'Holy, holy, holy is the Lord God Almighty, who was, and who is, and who is to come.'"

- *1 Peter 1:16:* "Be holy in all that you do; for I am holy."

9. Merciful (Compassionate)

God is compassionate and merciful to those who seek Him.

- *Psalm 103:8:* "The Lord is compassionate and gracious, slow to anger, abounding in love."

- *Psalm 130:7:* "O Israel, put your hope in the Lord; for with the Lord is unfailing love and with him is full redemption."

- *Jeremiah 31:3:* "For I have loved you with an everlasting love, therefore with lovingkindness I have drawn you and after I have drawn you I have continued My love to you."

10. Loving (Affectionate)

God is loving and affectionate towards those who are His children.

- *John 3:16:* "For God so loved the world that he gave his one and only Son, that whoever believes in him shall not perish but have eternal life."

- *1 John 4:16:* "And so we know and rely on the love God has for us. God is love. Whoever lives in love lives in God, and God in him."

- *Ephesians 2:4-5:* "But God, being rich in mercy, because of his great love for us, with which he loved us even when we were dead in our transgressions, made us live with Christ, whether we were alive or dead."

ATTRIBUTES OF JESUS

1. Life (John 1:4; 14:6)

Because of Jesus, we can now receive the gift of eternal life. This kind of life can only be given by one who oneself is eternal.

> *"In him was life, and that life was the light of men."*
>
> — JOHN 1:4

> *"Jesus told him, "I am the way, the truth, and the life. No one comes to the Father except through me. If you know me, you will also know my Father. From now on you do know him and have seen him."*
>
> — JOHN 14:6

2. Self-existence (John 5:26; Hebrews 7:16)

This means that Christ was uncreated and exists by himself alone, an attribute that only God could hold.

> *"For just as the Father has life in himself, so also he has granted to the Son to have life in himself."*
>
> — JOHN 5:26

> *"... who did not become a priest based on a legal regulation about physical descent but based on the power of an indestructible life."*
>
> — HEBREWS 7:16

3. Immutability (Hebrews 13:8)

Immutability means that one is unchangeable. While finite beings can and do change, a necessary infinite being does not.

> *"Jesus Christ is the same yesterday, today, and forever."*
>
> — HEBREWS 13:8

4. Truth (John 14:6; Revelation 3:7)

Titus 1:2 notes that God cannot lie. It is not that God chooses not to lie, but rather that he cannot because it goes against his nature. To claim that God is truth means that God's essence is sheer truth and possesses no falsehood. Scripture notes that Jesus holds this attribute.

> *"Jesus told him, "I am the way, the truth, and the life. No one comes to the Father except through me. If you know me, you will also know my Father. From now on you do know him and have seen him."*
>
> — JOHN 14:6

> *"Write to the angel of the church in Philadelphia: Thus says the Holy One, the true one, the one who has the key of David, who opens and no one will close, and who closes and no one opens."*
>
> — REVELATION 3:7

5. Love (1 John 3:16)

God is understood to be omnibenevolent; that is, all-loving. In God, there is no hate if he can be said to be absolute love. Theologians understand that God's wrath is rooted in God's love and his holiness. Scripture notes that Jesus holds the divine attribute of love.

> *"This is how we have come to know love: He laid down his life for us. We should also lay down our lives for our brothers and sisters."*
>
> — JOHN 3:16

6. Holiness (Luke 1:35; John 6:69; Hebrews 7:26)

God is absolutely holy. Absolute holiness is an all-encompassing purity, in which no evil is possessed. In other words, God is the absolute good. Scripture claims that Jesus holds this divine attribute of holiness which is necessary if he is to redeem humanity from their sin.

> *"The angel replied to her: "The Holy Spirit will come upon you, and the power of the Most High will overshadow you. Therefore, the holy one to be born will be called the Son of God."*
>
> — LUKE 1:35

> *"We have come to believe and know that you are the Holy One of God."*
>
> — JOHN 6:69

> *"For this is the kind of high priest we need: holy, innocent, undefiled, separated from sinners, and exalted above the heavens."*
>
> — HEBREWS 7:26

7. Eternity (John 1:1)

God is understood to be eternal. He has no beginning and no end. The Messiah is said to hold the same eternal attribute.

> *"Bethlehem Ephrathah, you are small among the clans of Judah; one will come from you to be ruler over Israel for me. His origin is from antiquity, from ancient times."*
>
> — MICAH 5:2

> *"In the beginning was the Word, and the Word was with God, and the Word was God."*
>
> — JOHN 1:1

8. Omnipresence (Matthew 28:20; Ephesians 1:23)

Omnipresence is the divine ability of God to be everywhere at all times. While Jesus did become monopresent during his time on earth, he is said to have the divine attribute of omnipresence in his eternal state.

> *"And remember, I am with you always, to the end of the age."*
>
> — MATTHEW 28:20

> *"And he subjected everything under his feet and appointed him as head over everything for the church, which is his body, the fullness of the one who fills all things in every way."*
>
> — EPHESIANS 1:22-23

9. Omniscience (Matthew 9:4; John 2:24, 25; Acts 1:24; 1 Corinthians 4:5; Colossians 2:3)

Omniscience is the divine attribute of God to know all things. This is an extremely deep concept as God knows all things that could be by his natural knowledge, all things that will be by his free knowledge, and all things that would be by his middle knowledge. Jesus is omniscient.

> *"Perceiving their thoughts, Jesus said, "Why are you thinking evil things in your hearts?"*
>
> — MATTHEW 9:4-5

> *"Jesus, however, would not entrust himself to them, since he knew them all and because he did not need anyone to testify about man; for he himself knew what was in man."*
>
> — JOHN 2:24-25

> *"Then they prayed, "You, Lord, know everyone's hearts; show which of these two you have chosen to take the place in this apostolic ministry that Judas left to go where he belongs."*
>
> — ACTS 1:24-25

> *"So don't judge anything prematurely, before the Lord comes, who will both bring to light what is hidden in darkness and reveal the intentions of the hearts. And then praise will come to each one from God."*
>
> — 1 CORINTHIANS 4:5

> *"In him are hidden all the treasures of wisdom and knowledge."*
>
> — COLOSSIANS 2:3

10. Omnipotence (Matthew 28:18; Revelation 1:8)

Omnipotence is the divine attribute of God that indicates God's complete power. God has complete authority and ultimate strength. Jesus holds the same attribute.

> *"All authority has been given to me in heaven and on earth."*
>
> — MATTHEW 28:18

> *"I am the Alpha and the Omega," says the Lord God, "the one who is, who was, and who is to come, the Almighty."*
>
> — REVELATION 1:8

ATTRIBUTES OF THE HOLY SPIRIT

He is fully God, equal in power and glory to the Father and the Son. The Holy Spirit is often described as a Comforter, Counselor, and Guide, sent to empower believers, give spiritual gifts, instruct in all wisdom, and bring conviction of sin. Scripture also associates the Holy Spirit with various symbols, such as fire, wind, and a dove.

1. Eternality: He has no beginning nor end. He existed before creation and will continue to exist forever.

2. Omnipresence: He is always present. He is everywhere at all times and not limited by space or time.

3. Omniscience: He is all-knowing. He knows all things, past, present, and future.

4. Omnipotence: He is all-powerful. He has the ability to do anything.

5. All Spirit: The Holy Spirit is spirit, not a physical being.

- *He speaks*: The Holy Spirit speaks to individuals and to the church as a whole. He guides, convicts, and instructs.
- *He can be grieved*: The Holy Spirit can be grieved by sin.
- *He intercedes*: The Holy Spirit intercedes for believers before God.
- *He searches:* The Holy Spirit searches the hearts and minds of people.
- *He has a mind*: The Holy Spirit has thoughts and intentions.
- *He has a will*: The Holy Spirit has His own will and purpose.

The Holy Spirit actively works in our lives by making known the presence of Jesus, shaping us to be more like Him, helping us understand Scripture, calling us to serve, empowering us for ministry and evangelism, helping us pray, guiding us, and giving us spiritual gifts.

Rather than overlooking the Holy Spirit, let us embrace His attributes and who He is as part of the Trinity, learning to walk more closely with Him. I hope this blog has helped you better understand who the Holy Spirit is and how He works in your life.

THE SACRIFICE VS. THE SACRIFICES

One God exists as three distinct Persons in the Trinity. Please note that this does not imply the existence of three Gods. The word "Trinity" does not appear in Scripture; however, it is used to describe the triune God—three coexisting, coeternal Persons who are one God. While the term itself is absent from the Bible, the reality it conveys is present throughout Scripture. God's Word affirms the following concerning the Trinity:

According to Leviticus 4:35 and 5:10, God required animal sacrifices as a means of atonement for sins and as a foreshadowing of the sinless death of Jesus Christ. The idea of animal sacrifice is significant and appears frequently in the Bible because, as Hebrews 9:22 states,

> *"There is no forgiveness without the shedding of blood."*
>
> — HEBREWS 9:22

Animals were sacrificed by God to provide clothing for Adam and Eve after their fall (Genesis 3:21). Noah also offered animals as sacrifices after the flood (Genesis 8:20–21). God gave the nation of Israel specific instructions to offer numerous sacrifices according to the laws He established. These sacrifices provided temporary covering for sin when offered in faith.

The sacrifices required on the Day of Atonement, described in Leviticus 16, further demonstrate forgiveness and the removal of sin. For the sin offering, the high priest was instructed to bring two male goats. One goat was sacrificed as the sin offering (Leviticus 16:15), while the other was released into the wilderness (Leviticus 16:20–22). The sacrificed goat symbolized forgiveness, while the released goat symbolized the removal of sin.

GOD SAW AND HE SPOKE

Many times, when we consider this topic, we do the opposite of what God modeled. We often wait to believe something *until* we see it, but in God's order, it is the speaking—what we first see in our minds—that brings things into the earth. The earth is fruitful because we are here. Humanity is here. God's creation is here.

The earth requires continuous tending. Creation is "groaning and moaning," waiting for the manifestation of the sons of God. The earth was designed to produce, so when it is not producing, it is similar to us experiencing an empty stomach and hunger pains. The earth has "hunger pains" when we are not fruitful. The earth is meant to produce continually, which is why we have seasons. Each season brings forth its own kind of production. It is almost as if the earth takes a break from producing certain things at certain times so there can be a continuous, orderly flow.

The earth produces different things in different seasons.

Summer:

- Fruits, such as watermelons, peaches, berries, and cantaloupe
- Vegetables, such as corn, tomatoes, zucchini, cucumbers, and peppers
- Flowers, such as sunflowers, roses, and daisies
- Grains, such as wheat, oats, and barley

Fall:

- Fruits, such as apples, pears, pumpkins, and grapes
- Vegetables, such as squash, sweet potatoes, and carrots
- Nuts, such as acorns, chestnuts, and walnuts
- Leaves changing colors and falling from trees

Winter:

- Snow and ice in some areas
- Trees are bare
- Evergreen trees produce pinecones
- In warmer climates, crops such as wheat and barley continue to grow

Spring:

- Flowers, such as daffodils, tulips, and azaleas
- Trees and plants begin to bud and grow leaves

- Vegetables, such as asparagus, peas, and lettuce
- Fruits, such as strawberries and cherries begin to ripen

Every season serves a purpose. And what all seasons have in common is this: *they are producing something.* I want to encourage you—no matter what season you are in, something is being produced in your life.

Think of what you deposit into the earth like a person depositing money into a bank. With a checking account, you withdraw what you put in immediately. But with a savings account, interest accrues, and you receive more than you deposited. In the same way, there are deposits—both good and bad—that have been made in the earth. We can either benefit from them or be hindered by them. Yet if we are covered by the blood of Jesus, we can benefit from them all, because God makes all things work together for good to those who love Him and are called according to His purpose.

Are you making good on the investment God has placed inside you? Consider the simple movement of your hands—something God gave us that benefits us daily. Think also of the seed planted in your heart regarding ministry or business. It may not be happening yet, but the seed has been planted. As you prepare and water that seed with the Word of God, you can expect it to materialize in due time.

CHAPTER 6
GOD'S DIVINE PLAN

God shows us His divine plan in the form of dreams and visions, which are formulated in our minds. This is why the mind should be a safe zone for every person. Here are some Scriptures concerning the mind. Make these your daily declarations over your mind:

- *Philippians 4:8* - "Finally, brothers and sisters, whatever is true, whatever is noble, whatever is right, whatever is pure, whatever is lovely, whatever is admirable—if anything is excellent or praiseworthy—think about such things."

- *Proverbs 4:23* - "Above all else, guard your heart, for everything you do flows from it."

- *Romans 12:2* - "Do not conform to the pattern of this world, but be transformed by the renewing of your mind. Then you will be able to test and approve what God's will is—his good, pleasing and perfect will."

- *1 Peter 1:13* - "Therefore, with minds that are alert and fully sober, set your hope on the grace to be brought to you when Jesus Christ is revealed at his coming."

- *Colossians 3:2* - "Set your minds on things above, not on earthly things."

- *Isaiah 26:3* - "You will keep in perfect peace those whose minds are steadfast, because they trust in you."

- *2 Corinthians 10:5* - "We demolish arguments and every pretension that sets itself up against the knowledge of God, and we take captive every thought to make it obedient to Christ."

- *Proverbs 3:5-6* - "Trust in the Lord with all your heart and lean not on your own understanding; in all your ways submit to him, and he will make your paths straight."

- *Psalm 119:105* - "Your word is a lamp for my feet, a light on my path."

- *Ephesians 4:23-24* - "to be made new in the attitude of your minds; and to put on the new self, created to be like God in true righteousness and holiness."

GUARDING YOUR MIND

How do you safeguard your mind? Guarding your mind according to the Bible involves actively protecting your thoughts and attitudes from anything that could negatively influence your relationship with God. Some ways to do this include:

1. Filling your mind with God's Word: The Word of God is the ultimate source of truth and wisdom. By studying it regularly and memorizing key verses, you can train your mind to think more like Christ.

2. Surrounding yourself with positive influences: Being around people who encourage you in your faith and help you focus on godly things can be a powerful way to guard your mind against negativity and temptation.

3. Avoiding negative influences: This includes things like violent or explicit media, negative or toxic relationships, or anything else that could drag you down spiritually.

4. Praying for spiritual protection: Asking God to help you guard your mind, protect you from negative influences, and guide your thoughts and actions is a powerful way to stay focused on Him.

5. Being aware of your thoughts: Pay attention to the thoughts running through your mind and intentionally redirect them when necessary. When negative or sinful thoughts arise, turn to prayer and Scripture to overcome them.

6. Focusing on gratitude: One way to guard your mind against negativity is to intentionally focus on the blessings in your life and express gratitude for them. This helps maintain a positive outlook and keeps your thoughts centered on God's goodness.

Also, the earth was simply an open space—darkness—but there was no evil present during this time. Darkness was not related to evil. God wanted to reveal that in the beginning, all things created by Him were without evil intent.

CRYSTAL LOVE

> *"And the Spirit of God was hovering over the face of the waters."*
>
> — GENESIS 1:2

As I read this, I pictured the Spirit of God looking as though He were facing a mirror. But notice that the earth was without form, so where was the water? Was there a bottom to the water? Was the water suspended in midair? The water was the first thing that did not have to be spoken; it already existed.

The Holy Spirit and His symbolic meaning as water relates to baptism, according to Matthew 3:11:

> *"I baptize you with water for repentance. But after me will come One who is more powerful than I, whose sandals I am not fit to carry."*
>
> — MATTHEW 3:11

Then, we read in Acts,

> *John baptized with water, but in just a few days you will be baptized with the Holy Spirit.*
>
> — ACTS 1:5

In Genesis 2, we see the need for water, which was used to water the Garden of God—the garden of life—through a supernatural occurrence. On earth, when we water a garden, we nurture the seed so it can become what it was created to be. We are the farmers tending the garden, while God oversees it all. He governs it, and He teaches us through the Holy Spirit how to maintain our gardens called life. Water symbolizes life, and it also represents the Holy Spirit. When the believer is filled with the Holy Spirit and led by Him, they enter into a new life.

Genesis 1:20 says,

> *"Let the waters abound with an abundance of living creatures, and let birds fly above the earth across the face of the firmament (sky) of the heavens."*
>
> — GENESIS 1:20

Earlier, God said, "Let there be light," and there was light. God saw the light, and it was good; and God divided the light from the darkness. This is when time was created, because the next verse says, "God called the light Day, and the darkness He called Night. So the evening and the morning were the first day." Here we see the division of light from darkness. There was—and is—a purpose for darkness. It helps us rest and tells us when to rise. There is purpose in everything, and darkness carries many significances.

Next, in verses 6–8, the waters are divided. While division is often negative—especially when God calls His people to unity—here we see that certain distinctions and classifications were necessary so that order could be established. Satan's expulsion from heaven occurred sometime between creation and the garden, because God commanded Adam and Eve not to eat from the tree of the knowledge of good and evil. Evil was already present, but not within them.

Whatever you partner with becomes one with you. You enter covenant agreement with whatever you believe and act upon. When we believe that Jesus Christ died for our sins and confess our sins, we are born again and enter covenant with God and the work of the cross. Likewise, when we come into agreement with the devil's lies, sin is conceived.

> *"After desire has conceived, it gives birth to sin; and sin, when it is full-grown, gives birth to death."*
>
> — JAMES 1:15

CRYSTAL LOVE

Temptation can lead to sin, but it doesn't have to. It is wise to remember that whenever you are tempted.

> *"How you have fallen from heaven, morning star, son of the dawn! You have been cast down to the earth, you who once laid low the nations! You said in your heart, 'I will ascend to the heavens;*
> *I will raise my throne above the stars of God;*
> *I will sit enthroned on the mount of assembly, on the utmost heights of Mount Zaphon. I will ascend above the tops of the clouds; I will make myself like the Most High."*
>
> — ISAIAH 14:12–14

> *"Son of man, take up a lament concerning the king of Tyre and say to him: 'This is what the Sovereign Lord says:*
> *'You were the seal of perfection,*
> *full of wisdom and perfect in beauty.*
> *You were in Eden,*
> *the garden of God;*
> *every precious stone adorned you:*
> *carnelian, chrysolite and emerald,*
> *topaz, onyx and jasper,*
> *lapis lazuli, turquoise and beryl.*
> *Your settings and mountings were made of gold;*
> *on the day you were created they were prepared.*
> *You were anointed as a guardian cherub,*
> *for so I ordained you.*
> *You were on the holy mount of God;*
> *you walked among the fiery stones.*
> *You were blameless in your ways*
> *from the day you were created*
> *till wickedness was found in you.*
> *Through your widespread trade*
> *you were filled with violence,*

and you sinned.
So I drove you in disgrace from the mount of God,
and I expelled you, guardian cherub,
from among the fiery stones.
Your heart became proud
on account of your beauty,
and you corrupted your wisdom
because of your splendor.
So I threw you to the earth;
I made a spectacle of you before kings.
By your many sins and dishonest trade
you have desecrated your sanctuaries.
So I made a fire come out from you,
and it consumed you,
and I reduced you to ashes on the ground
in the sight of all who were watching.'"

— EZEKIEL 28:12–18

While these two passages are referring specifically to the kings of Babylon and Tyre, we believe they also reference the spiritual power behind those kings, namely, Satan. These passages describe *why* Satan fell, but they do not say *when* the fall occurred.

Jesus, the eternal Son of God, witnessed Satan's fall, and He mentions it in Luke 10:18:

"I saw Satan fall like lightning from heaven." We know that the angels were created before the earth."

— LUKE 10:18

"Where were you when I laid the foundation of the earth? Tell me, if you have understanding. Who determined its measurements—surely you know! Or who stretched the line upon it? On what were its bases sunk, or who laid its

cornerstone, when the morning stars sang together and all the sons of God shouted for joy?"

— JOB 38:4–7

Satan fell before he tempted Adam and Eve in the garden (*Genesis 3:1–14*). His fall, therefore, must have occurred sometime after the angels were created and before he tempted Adam and Eve in the Garden of Eden.

As we look further at God's creation and the order in which He established all things, we must talk about order. First, let us notice the word *create*, which we previously defined as: to form or fashion, to produce, to carve or cut out, to bring into existence, or to fashion something new from what already exists. God did this when He created man according to Genesis 1:27, forming him from the dust of the ground so He could take something divine and create something in its natural form.

CHAPTER 7
GOD'S DIVINE ORDER

As we look in the Scriptures, we find that God often shows us what the end will look like in the spirit realm, and then we have to come back to reality and walk it out. This gives us confidence, knowing that the end is supposed to look a specific way. I believe the controversy comes in when we start asking how we are going to make what God showed us happen.

We must never think that we can create what God has already created and revealed. If you look at the order of how He created everything, it was all the result of a future need. If God has already created it, all we have to do is call it forth from heaven into the earth. We pray from a place of dominion, not from a place of lack.

Let's take a look back at *Genesis* chapter 1, going up a little farther. What are some necessities of light? Let's name a few.

LIGHT

1. Vision: Light is necessary for humans to see and perceive their surroundings. Without light, everything would be pitch black, and it would be impossible to see anything.

2. Health: Exposure to natural light is beneficial for human health, as it helps regulate our circadian rhythm, our internal clock that controls the sleep–wake cycle.

3. Safety: Adequate lighting is necessary for safety, especially in public spaces. Good lighting can help prevent accidents and crimes.

4. Productivity: Adequate lighting is essential for productivity in both home and work environments. Poor lighting can cause eye strain and fatigue, which can lead to decreased efficiency and productivity.

5. Mood: Light can affect our mood and emotional state. Bright light can boost our mood and energy levels, while dim lighting can create a cozy and relaxing atmosphere.

The primary source of light during the day is the sun. The sun is a star located at the center of the solar system and is responsible for providing light and heat to the earth. Light from the sun travels through space and reaches the earth, where it illuminates the planet and enables photosynthesis in plants, which is essential for the survival of most life forms on the planet.

The sun is essential for life on earth and provides various benefits, including:

1. Light: The sun is the primary source of light for the earth. Sunlight helps plants grow and provides warmth for animals and humans.

2. Energy: The sun's energy is used to generate electricity through solar panels, which is a renewable and sustainable source of energy.

3. Vitamin D: Sun exposure helps the body produce vitamin D, which is essential for strong bones, teeth, and overall health.

4. Climate: The sun helps regulate the earth's climate by providing heat, which drives weather patterns and ocean currents.

5. Photosynthesis: Plants use the sun's energy to convert carbon dioxide into oxygen through photosynthesis, which is critical for the earth's ecosystem.

The sun is a vital component of life on earth and plays a crucial role in sustaining our planet's ecosystem.

> "Then God said, let the earth bring forth grass, the herb that yields seed and a fruit tree that yields fruit according to its kind, whose seed is in its self on the earth and it was so. And the earth brought forth grass, the herb that yields seed, according to its kind, and the tree that yields fruit whose seed is in its self, according to its kind. And God saw that it was good."
>
> — GENESIS 1:11-12

The grass, the seed, the fruit, and the tree all need light. God had already provided for this so that these things He created later would be preserved and would continue to produce through one essential element: light.

So, let's explain in detail how the light, which is the sun, nurtures grass, seeds, fruit, and trees.

The light from the sun is essential for the process of photosynthesis, which is how plants produce their food. During photosynthesis, plants use the energy from sunlight to convert carbon dioxide and water into glucose and oxygen. This process takes place in the chloroplasts, which are specialized structures within plant cells containing chlorophyll, the pigment that gives plants their green color.

When sunlight hits a leaf, the chlorophyll in the chloroplasts absorbs some of the energy from the light. This energy is then used to split water molecules into oxygen and hydrogen ions, which are used to produce ATP, a molecule that stores energy. The ATP is then used to power the conversion of carbon dioxide into glucose, which is stored in the plant's cells as food.

This process is essential for the growth and survival of plants, and it also has a significant impact on the environment. The oxygen produced during photosynthesis is released into the atmosphere, where it is used by animals and humans for respiration. The carbon dioxide taken in by plants during photosynthesis is also an important greenhouse gas, which helps regulate the earth's temperature.

DARKNESS

Darkness can be defined as the absence or lack of light, resulting in a dim or completely dark environment. The Bible has a lot to say about darkness.

The Oxford Dictionary defines darkness as the partial or total absence of light, or wickedness/evil. In Hebrew, however, the word for darkness is *khoshek*. The *Strong's* reference says this word is used 78 times in the Bible and means one of three things: darkness/obscurity, darkness, or a secret place. Interestingly, *Strong's* also notes the Greek word *skotos*, which means "the principle of sin with its certain results."

As we see here, the world was void and dark. Darkness existed before light. Nothing in the text says the darkness was bad—only that it existed—until God created light. Light and darkness were both necessary in God's creation for the earth and the universe to function as He intended. Light balanced the darkness, and God never removed or expelled darkness altogether. Darkness is needed as much as light for the planets to function in God's design. I am led to believe that darkness, in and of itself, is not evil.

> *"Then God made two great lights, the greater light to rule the day, and the lesser light to rule the night. He made the stars also. God set them in the firmament of the heavens, to give light on the earth, and to rule over the day and over the night, and to divide the light from the darkness, and God saw that it was good."*
>
> — GENESIS 1:16-18

God made two great lights: the greater light to rule the day and the lesser light to rule the night—so we would not be in total darkness. As it relates to the spirit realm, we are totally oblivious to the things of God when we are not illuminated by the Holy Spirit. The "greater light" is commonly accepted as the sun, and the "lesser light" to the moon.

STARS

According to Genesis 1:14–15, it is written that God created the stars "to separate the day from the night" and "to serve as signs to mark seasons and days and years." The stars have also been used for navigation and to guide travelers.

> *"Now when Jesus was born in Bethlehem of Judaea in the days of Herod the king, behold, there came wise men from the east to Jerusalem,*
> *Saying, Where is he that is born King of the Jews? for we have seen his star in the east, and are come to worship him.*
> *When Herod the king had heard these things, he was troubled, and all Jerusalem with him.*
> *And when he had gathered all the chief priests and scribes of the people together, he demanded of them where Christ should be born.*
> *And they said unto him, In Bethlehem of Judaea: for thus it is written by the prophet,*

*And thou Bethlehem, in the land of Juda, art not the least
among the princes of Juda: for out of thee shall come a
Governor, that shall rule my people Israel.
Then Herod, when he had privily called the wise men,
enquired of them diligently what time the star appeared.
And he sent them to Bethlehem, and said, Go and search diligently for the young child; and when ye have found him,
bring me word again, that I may come and worship him
also.
When they had heard the king, they departed; and, lo, the star,
which they saw in the east, went before them, till it came
and stood over where the young child was.
When they saw the star, they rejoiced with exceeding great
joy."*

— MATTHEW 2:1–10

Some scholars and theologians believe that the wise men may have been studying the stars and prophecies for years, waiting for a sign to indicate the birth of a great king. When they saw the star, they understood it as a sign that the King of the Jews had been born and followed it to find Jesus. It is also possible that they did not immediately know the significance of the star and had to inquire further to understand its meaning.

The wise men, or magi, were eastern astrologers. Astrology was a sophisticated science in that era. As trained students of the stars, the wise men observed an unexplained phenomenon in the heavens, which they interpreted as a sign of the birth of the King of the Jews.

However, the Bible warns against divination, sorcery, and consulting mediums—practices commonly associated with astrology in ancient times.

*"There shall not be found among you anyone who... practices
witchcraft, or a soothsayer, or one who interprets omens, or
a sorcerer, or one who conjures spells, or a medium, or a*

spiritist, or one who calls up the dead. For all who do these things are an abomination to the Lord."

— DEUTERONOMY 18:10–12

Followers of Christ are advised to seek guidance and direction from God through prayer, reading the Bible, and seeking wise counsel, rather than relying on astrological readings or other forms of divination.

*"Trust in the Lord with all your heart
and lean not on your own understanding;
in all your ways submit to him,
and he will make your paths straight."*

— PROVERBS 3:5–6

"If any of you lacks wisdom, you should ask God, who gives generously to all without finding fault, and it will be given to you."

— JAMES 1:5

To go further, Genesis 1:17 says God "set them in the firmament of the heavens, to give light on the earth, and to rule over the day and over the night, and to divide the light from the darkness."

FIRMAMENT

The term *firmament* is used in the Bible to describe the expanse or the heavens above the earth. In the creation story in Genesis 1:6–8, it is described as a firmament separating the waters above from the waters below—like a dome-like expanse between earth and the heavens. The word "firmament" comes from the Latin *firmamentum*, meaning "a support" or "foundation," and was used to describe the heavenly vault that was believed to support the stars, sun, and moon.

The firmament is the vast dome created by God in the *Genesis* narrative to divide the primal sea into upper and lower portions so that dry land could appear.

WATER

The percentage of water on earth is about 71%, with the remaining 29% being land. The percentage of water in the heavens is much lower and difficult to quantify. Water is relatively rare in the universe, and its presence depends on many factors, including temperature, pressure, and the presence of other elements and compounds. Some estimates suggest that water makes up less than 0.05% of the total mass of the observable universe. Our understanding of the universe is still developing, so exact percentages are difficult to determine.

Water in the sky exists largely in the form of water vapor, an invisible gas formed when water evaporates from bodies of water, plants, and other surfaces. When the air cools, water vapor can condense into visible clouds or fog.

LAND

> *"Then God said, Let the waters under the heavens be gathered together into one place, and let the dry land appear; and it was so. And God called the dry land Earth, and the gathering together of the waters He called Seas. And God saw that it was good.*
> *Then God said, Let the earth bring forth grass, the herb that yields seed, and the fruit tree that yields fruit according to its kind, whose seed is in itself, on the earth; and it was so."*
>
> — GENESIS 1:9–11

Take a moment to imagine how much water that must have been, and how it was displaced. Because God is God, there was still order in where the water was and how it moved. To the natural eye it may have looked condensed, but this was a supernatural moment in time when the earth and its foundations were being set in place. We can, to a certain extent, try to make sense of it, but we must also remember that no one can fully know the depths of God.

> *"For who among men knows the thoughts of a man except the man's spirit within him? In the same way no one knows the thoughts of God except the Spirit of God.*
> *We have not received the spirit of the world but the Spirit who is from God, that we may understand what God has freely given us. This is what we speak, not in words taught us by human wisdom but in words taught by the Spirit, expressing spiritual truths in spiritual words.*
> *The man without the Spirit does not accept the things that come from the Spirit of God, for they are foolishness to him, and he cannot understand them, because they are spiritually discerned.*
> *The spiritual man makes judgments about all things, but he himself is not subject to any man's judgment:*
> *For who has known the mind of the Lord that he may instruct him? But we have the mind of Christ."*
>
> — 1 CORINTHIANS 2:11–16

We are limited by human wisdom, and if God so chooses to reveal to us the depth of what He has done thousands of years ago, it is a humbling gift to receive the mysteries of God.

> *"He reveals mysteries from the darkness and brings the deep darkness into light."*
>
> — JOB 12:22

Even in a dark place, the mysteries of God can be revealed when we are illuminated by the light of God. Another wave of understanding interrupts our natural way of thinking.

> *"There was the true Light which, coming into the world, enlightens every man."*
>
> — JOHN 1:9

There was darkness before God spoke light, and after light came, everything else in creation was established. Light had to be revealed first.

Creation and revelation go hand in hand. When you receive revelation from God—something that was once hidden but is now shown to you—it is your responsibility to reveal it in whatever manner God instructs. When you reveal what God had concealed, He creates and reproduces that truth over and over again. This is why the devil does not want us to seek God, hear what He says, understand what He reveals, and release what He speaks.

The true Light enlightens every person. But enlightenment alone does not bring change; the *choice*, made through faith, produces change. You are enlightened to the truth so that you can make a decision to walk in that truth. You can be aware of danger, see it clearly, and still choose to walk into it. That is what deception does. You are enlightened enough to choose to follow God, and then He begins to reveal the things of God to you. The rest of the revelation comes by faith. You will not be able to contain the fullness of it if you remain in a place of indecision. The verse below explains this even more:

> *"It is He who reveals the profound and hidden things;*
> *He knows what is in the darkness,*
> *And the light dwells with Him."*
>
> — DANIEL 2:22

He reveals profound and hidden things. *Profound* means having or showing great knowledge or insight.

> *"I press on toward the goal for the prize of the upward call of God in Christ Jesus.*
> *Let those of us who are mature think this way, and if in anything you think otherwise, God will reveal that also to you."*
>
> — PHILIPPIANS 3:14–15

The upward call is a progression; it unfolds as you walk out your journey as a born-again believer. Verse 15 speaks of maturity—for those who are mature in their walk. There is no set amount of time required; it is up to the believer, and their pursuit of God, that determines how far they go in Him. It is truly a press.

> *"Blessed are they that hunger and thirst after righteousness, for they shall be filled."*
>
> — MATTHEW 5:6

It is all based on your hunger and thirst.

> *"You, God, are my God, earnestly I seek you; I thirst for you, my whole being longs for you, in a dry and parched land where there is no water."*
>
> — PSALM 63:1

Our spirit man is dead before we give our lives to Christ. The Bible tells us, "For the wages of sin is death; but the gift of God is eternal life through Jesus Christ our Lord" (*Romans 6:23*). So we are "living dead" without God. We do not truly begin to walk in our purpose until we are born again.

God wants us to live out eternity with Christ—that is life. Sin is death. The "dry and parched land" is natural life without a supernatural walk with God.

> *"but whoever drinks of the water that I will give him shall never thirst; but the water that I will give him will become in him a well of water springing up to eternal life."*
>
> — JOHN 4:14

"Springing up" is where the takeover begins. The water never runs dry because we live there. God is our source of life. He is our life. He knows everything about our lives.

So when we stay in the presence of God every day—you can walk out your entire day with the Lord: being a mother, a father, taking care of your children, running a business, pastoring a church, being a CEO, gardening, grocery shopping—everyday life on earth can still be lived while walking with God. Our spirit man never sleeps, so even while our body is resting at night, our spirit is being fed. When you keep the channel open with God in the spirit realm, there will always be a flow of Him imparting and you receiving what He is trying to get to you and flow through you in the earth. It is beneficial for us to remain open.

How do we remain open to God and all that He has for us?

1. Prayer: Communication with God, either through spoken words or inner thoughts—asking for guidance, forgiveness, or expressing gratitude.

2. Worship: Expressing reverence and adoration toward God through singing, dancing, serving, and other acts that acknowledge His worthiness and majesty.

3. Studying the Word of God: Exploring and understanding the

Bible to gain knowledge and wisdom about God's character, His plan, and His teachings for living a righteous life.

4. Fasting: Refraining from food or other activities for a set period to deepen one's spiritual connection with God, seek direction, and discipline the body and mind.

5. Living a consecrated life: Living a life set apart for God's purposes, characterized by obedience to His will, holiness, and service to others.

6. Meditating on the Word: Reflecting deeply on Scripture, contemplating its implications, and seeking to apply its truths to daily life with God.

> *"Ask and it will be given to you; seek and you will find; knock and the door will be opened to you. For everyone who asks receives; he who seeks finds; and to him who knocks, the door will be opened."*
>
> — MATTHEW 7:7

Hunger and thirst for God are based on the individual. It is truly a choice. But if you are being transformed by the renewing of your mind—by sowing seeds into the garden of your heart—you will benefit from it. Knowing what is right and knowing how to do what is right can be two different challenges. This is why the Holy Spirit teaches us all things.

> *"Let those of us who are mature think this way, and if in anything you think otherwise, God will reveal that also to you."*
>
> — PHILIPPIANS 3:15

The more you are filled with Him—which means your capacity to receive increases—the more you will yearn to please Him and flow in His ways. We are human and divine; the spirit man must be fortified to resist the pull of the flesh. The more you receive in the spirit, the less you yield to the flesh. He fills you with Himself. The more you die to your fleshly desires, the more you yield to His control. The more you feed your spirit and grow, the stronger you become to withstand temptation.

It is like a balance scale: the more you invest in one side, the stronger it becomes. The Spirit of God is strong in Himself; it is your yielding to the Spirit that makes you strong in Him. He gives you the willpower to advance in every area of your life.

Whenever you begin to think about things you should not be thinking—things not in alignment with the Holy Spirit—the Holy Spirit will let you know and steer you back in the right direction. You cannot go wrong with the leading of the Holy Spirit.

CHAPTER 8
THE COMFORTER

Why is the Holy Spirit considered a comforter? Think about this question. Don't you find comfort when you feel secure? What makes you uncomfortable? Uncomfortability can come when something unfamiliar is right in our faces —when we don't know what's next.

So, when we know the purpose of the Holy Spirit, it does give us comfort, letting us know that we don't have to worry about what's next because the comforter, the Holy Spirit, will let us know that everything is already all right because God knows the totality of our entire life.

So, when we are uncertain, we can always find solace in God, knowing that we always win, we always come out on top because He is the author of everything. And if there is anything held back, He'll show us how to get in alignment with God. He'll show us what is holding us back from walking into what He promised for us.

There's nothing hidden with God, so as long as we have a comforter, we will be aware of what's ahead.

"I have told you all this so that you may have peace in me.

Here on earth you will have many trials and sorrows. But take heart, because I have overcome the world."

— JOHN 16:33

Because of the evil in the world in the fight that we are up against according to:

"For we wrestle not against flesh and blood, but against principalities, against powers, against the rulers of the darkness of this world, against spiritual wickedness in high places.

Wherefore take unto you the whole armour of God, that ye may be able to withstand in the evil day, and having done all, to stand."

— EPHESIANS 6:12-13

Here it is all in one scripture as to how we overcome, because He has overcome already. And we stay protected by putting on His armor.

"Like newborn infants, long for the pure spiritual milk, that by it you may grow up into salvation"

— 1 PETER 2:2

"Brothers, do not be children in your thinking. Be infants in evil, but in your thinking be mature."

— 1 CORINTHIANS 14:20

"Do not be conformed to this world, but be transformed by the renewal of your mind, that by testing you may discern

> *what is the will of God, what is good and acceptable and perfect."*
>
> — ROMANS 12:2

The later portion of the scripture says, "He shall teach you all things and bring all things to your remembrance, whatsoever I have said unto you." If it's a delay, God wants you to know that He's setting you up for the testimony. He said He's digging up the rubbish. In order to take us higher, He has to go deeper. You have to be anchored.

Hebrews 6:19–20 declares:

> *"The hope we have as an anchor of the soul, both sure and steadfast, and which enters the presence behind the veil, where the forerunner has entered for us, even Jesus, having become High Priest forever according to the order of Melchizedek."*
>
> — HEBREWS 6:19–20

An anchor is only as secure as that which it is fastened to. Anchoring may keep the vessel safely positioned head-on to heavy conditions, and it can also allow you to retain your position and not be swept away or pushed on shore. This has to happen before you can go deeper in God. I'm going to take you deeper in the water so that you can swim so deep that you can see the bottom. No more shallow water. Dive in. Take a deep breath and go under. God said, I'm strengthening you to swim in the water, anchored in Me, graced to carry the weight of glory that I allowed you to swim in. It's in the water you are consumed by the river of living water; all of who you are is consumed in it. You can find Me in the water. You can find Me consumed by the Holy Spirit. Oxygen is extracted from water in fish. God said all you need is in Me; you can't do this on your own.

CRYSTAL LOVE

> *"My people have committed two sins: They have forsaken me, the spring of living water, and have dug their own cisterns, broken cisterns that cannot hold water."*
>
> — JEREMIAH 2:13

> *"Whoever believes in me, as Scripture has said, rivers of living water will flow from within them."*
>
> — JOHN 7:38

Rivers are freshwater bodies of water that flow from higher elevations, such as mountains or hills, and eventually empty into larger bodies of water, such as lakes or oceans. Rivers flow from mountains or hills.

There are several instances where people went on a mountain to receive from God.

1. Moses received the Ten Commandments from God on Mount Sinai (Exodus 19–20).
2. Elijah received instructions and encouragement from God on Mount Horeb (1 Kings 19).
3. Jesus gave His famous Sermon on the Mount, where He taught His disciples about the Beatitudes and other important lessons (Matthew 5–7).

These are just a few examples, but there are many other instances in the Bible where mountains are significant locations for receiving guidance, inspiration, and messages from God. Rivers are typically fed by smaller streams or tributaries, and their flow is influenced by a variety of factors, including rainfall, snowmelt, and the geography of the surrounding landscape. Fed by smaller streams, which symbolizes intimacy with the Father. It's in the secret place where you receive a special touch from God—meaning to follow God in His shadow, to pursue God, a constant companion, intimate, close friend.

THE HOLY SPIRIT EXPLAINED

"He who dwells in the secret place of the Most High Shall abide under the shadow of the Almighty."

— PSALM 91:1

"When my glory passes by, I will put you in a cleft in the rock and cover you with my hand until I have passed by."

— EXODUS 33:22

Rainfall has a significant impact on river flow. When it rains, the water runs off the surface of the land and into nearby streams and rivers. This causes the river flow to increase. The more rainfall there is, the greater the river flow will be. In the natural, that is in the spirit. When you stay in the flow of God, saturated in the glory, the flow increases. Aren't you ready for the increase? Stay on the river; God never stops the flow. The outpour is constantly coming. He said, stay in my presence, covered by the shadow of my wings in a place of consistent intimacy with me, consistent pursuit of me, and it will constantly be a flow and overflow.

During periods of heavy rain, rivers can experience flash flooding. This is when the river flow increases rapidly, causing the water level to rise and potentially causing damage to nearby structures and communities. The world, the people that are connected to us, need a flooding of the power and the glory of God to take over, take them in so much, and so that it will cause damage to the kingdom of hell, to the kingdom of darkness. Every structure that was not built by God would be destroyed and overpowered by the glory of God.

And when it's time to build again, according to Nehemiah, the people gather together from places of shame, places of being in bondage, and being locked up in prison by their own past sins and past failures, and just the enemy throwing so many lies and convincing them that they are not ready and able to follow and do what God has called them to do, that God is unlocking the prison doors, and He is taking the chains off of His people so that they can walk in what God promised them to be, and be what God spoke over their lives to be.

I declare right now in the name of Jesus that there will be no more drought—why? Because you will stay in the water, stay saturated in the presence of God. Don't allow anything or anyone to cause you to leave. While some rivers do eventually empty into oceans, this river, because of your place of intimacy, will begin to empty out into oceans, which is a large body of water, because God said, I am going to use you to reach large masses of people. Because of what has been done in secret, God said He is rewarding it openly.

> "So that your giving may be in secret. Then your Father, who sees what is done in secret, will reward you."
>
> — MATTHEW 6:4

> "But the Comforter, who is the Holy Ghost whom the Father will send in My name, He shall teach you all things and bring all things to your remembrance, whatsoever I have said unto you."
>
> — JOHN 14:26

Why did they need comfort?

They were grieving the separation from Jesus. Someone who walked with them would no longer be present with them in the physical body. Pain and suffering would happen moving forward. God was not going to leave them hanging with no hope for the future and no help to endure what was going to happen in the future.

Power

> "But you will receive power when the Holy Spirit comes on

THE HOLY SPIRIT EXPLAINED

you; and you will be my witnesses in Jerusalem, and in all Judea and Samaria, and to the ends of the earth."

— ACTS 1:8

Demonstration

"When all the people were being baptized, Jesus was baptized too. And as he was praying, heaven was opened and the Holy Spirit descended on him in bodily form like a dove. And a voice came from heaven: 'You are my Son, whom I love; with you I am well pleased.'"

— LUKE 3:21–22

"Jesus went up on a mountainside and called to him those he wanted, and they came to him. He appointed twelve that they might be with him and that he might send them out to preach and to have authority to drive out demons."

— MARK 3:13–15 NIV

"But if I cast out devils by the Spirit of God, then the kingdom of God is come unto you."

— MATTHEW 12:28–50

The Promise

The night before Jesus was crucified, He told His disciples that He would be leaving them and that they could not go with Him (John 13:33). Peter asked where He was going and why they couldn't go with Him, and Jesus assured them that they would follow Him eventually (John 13:36–37). Jesus said,

> *"In my Father's house are many rooms. If it were not so, would I have told you that I go to prepare a place for you? And if I go and prepare a place for you, I will come again and will take you to myself, that where I am you may be also."*
>
> — JOHN 14:2–3

This saying of Jesus may be interpreted differently by many because of the King James Version's rendering of the words "house" and "mansions." The Greek word translated "house" means "an abode," literally or figuratively, and, by implication, "a family." The word translated "mansions" or "rooms" means literally "the act of staying or residing." So, putting the Greek together, Jesus is saying that in God's home (heaven) there will be many people in the family of God all abiding together. Within God's heavenly house, Christians will live in the presence of the Lord. This is quite different from the idea of rows of mansions on streets of gold, which is the image many people have of what Jesus was saying.

Jesus Christ prepares a place in heaven for His own, those who have come to Him in faith, and the Holy Spirit prepares the redeemed on earth for their place in heaven. Revelation 7:9 tells us that there will be a "great multitude in heaven that no one could number" all standing before the throne. Jesus was crucified at Passover time, and He ascended 40 days after His resurrection. The Holy Spirit came 50 days after the resurrection, 10 days after the ascension. Jews of many nations had gathered in Jerusalem to celebrate the festival. When the day of Pentecost came, they were all together in one place.

> *"But the Comforter, who is the Holy Ghost whom the Father will send in My name, He shall teach you all things and bring all things to your remembrance, whatsoever I have said unto you."*
>
> — JOHN 14:26

CHAPTER 9
PREDESTINATION

We are predestined, which means that everything that happens has already been determined by God—He has a master plan, and there is no deviating from it when you are fully submitted to Him. The Bible teaches both predestination and free will, and does not attempt to reconcile them, leaving this within the mystery of God Himself. Our lives are already set; we are already chosen by God, and at the appointed time we are presented with the choice to follow the predestined path into eternal glory or to choose the path that leads to eternal damnation.

In Ephesians 1, Paul wrote,

> *"He has let us know my story of His purpose, the hidden plan He so kindly made Christ from the beginning... We were claimed as God's own, chosen from the beginning under the predetermined plan of the One who guides all things as He decides by His own will."*
>
> — EPHESIANS 1:9-11

Prayer is a means to bring to pass that which God has determined shall be. When we pray, we are not hoping to alter God's eternal purposes; we are praying to obtain that outcome which God has ordained to be received by our prayers. Free will is the belief that people have the capacity to make decisions independently of God or any other external influence.

God's "election" of people is therefore based on their own faith-response to Him, and His grace can be either resisted or accepted—we can say "yes" or "no" to Him. Every human being, therefore, has a choice concerning his or her eternal destiny. When we are born again, we are opened to the reality of the work of blood of Jesus Christ that afforded us the life that was already planned out. So, now we accept the truth about everything that pertains to our lives now into this new life.

How is new life translated to me? It's just like having a translator who makes sense of things spoken in another language. The Holy Spirit is our translator; now that we have His Spirit, everything that comes across our ear gates and eye gates, and all our senses, will come with a different level of insight as time goes on, because our lives are now being translated to us.

Having this awareness opens us up to the vast world of opportunity called the spirit realm. Now we are walking and living in two worlds. Can that be confusing? Yet because God is not the author of confusion, the confused part of us is the humanity side that does not see the true meaning behind it all. It can only be translated and understood in the Spirit, and then our whole being can choose to obey. The main source of making this decision is full submission to God's plan for your life and allowing Him to walk you through it with guidance that you could not produce without assistance. Our maintenance manual is the Word of God.

How do you upkeep and upgrade who you are? By tapping into God's plan for you. That's the only way. People think that when you know people who know people, your life can upgrade. Your status can change in a matter of minutes depending on whom you know. But that is temporary and is released at times because God has given us favor with Him and with man, so you can soar in the totality of what life entails.

We make decisions based on what we perceive and understand to be fact, but as things open up more deeply, our decisions are ultimately based on what we believe; faith is your key component in this understanding.

I'm deciding to live forward in this area because I believe what God said. He promised something, and He gave you instructions to get to or get through to that promise. You have to get through the lies, deception, discontent, and dismiss the misinformation of the old mindset that is being renewed day by day by the transforming power of the Word of God. If you don't know the Word of God, your transformation process will be limited and will not reach its full capacity.

This is why, at times, you may witness that some people who have been saved for many years still have the same level of understanding they had in the early stages of their walk with God—it's because they weren't open to the possibilities of more. Are we open to the fact that there is a world we have yet to fully understand and interpret, and this world is the spirit world? This is the place we ought to live from. The Holy Spirit translates what we see and understand and applies it to the life we live from one world, applying the principles to both worlds.

Everyone's level of understanding is different, so patience is required to receive greater revelation. Patience and revelation work together. Sometimes you have to wait on your mind to catch up with what the spirit man has been trying to reveal the entire time. The human mind, without the translation of the mind of Christ, will try to rationalize what does not add up in the natural sense. In other words, "it doesn't make sense." Humanity wants to respond with words or actions when the Holy Spirit says, "Be still; keep silent." What we take in with understanding is what we release in wisdom.

Think of the Holy Spirit as the metal detector within. Everything that tries to enter must go through inspection to determine whether you're passing through, staying, or being immediately denied entry. What comes in takes residence and takes precedence—meaning priority in importance, order, or rank. Things that come in should be filed in folders of occupancy. What occupies your mind controls your life. Let this mind be in you that was also in Christ Jesus. The mind of Christ is imputed by way of the Holy Spirit and governs how we perceive life.

We have those in high rank who govern the world. God governs you from your eternal state. The president of the United States, the governors, and the mayors are only given a certain space of time to make an impact. No matter what position you hold or the time allotted, will you make it power-packed and filled with change that will last a lifetime into eternity? What we do now—yes, it follows us into eternity. What we do is translated to every generation behind us.

In eternity, Moses is who he is, and what he did continues to resound, meaning to give forth and proclaim. The transfiguration gives us a glimpse of this truth. "Transfiguration" means a complete change of form or appearance. Peter, James, and John were able to see Jesus differently because of their close proximity to Him. He was able to give them a revelation of who He was and is to God in one moment in time, bringing back Moses and Elijah, symbolizing the Law of the Old and the prophetic calling forth into the New with Elijah.

> "Six days later, Jesus took with Him Peter and James and his brother John and led them up a high mountain by themselves. And He was transfigured before them, and His face shone like the sun, and His clothes became dazzling white."
>
> — MATTHEW 17:1–2

> "While He was speaking, a cloud appeared and covered them, and they were afraid as they entered the cloud. A voice came from the cloud, saying, "This is my Son, whom I have chosen; listen to Him." When the voice had spoken, they found that Jesus was alone."
>
> — LUKE 9:34-35

The Bible says that out of two or three witnesses His Word will be established. Jesus is greater than Moses and Elijah. Some people mistook Jesus for Elijah, and others thought He called for Elijah from the cross (Mark 15:35). Elijah was a great prophet of the Lord in the Old Testament, and so was Moses. God led His people out of slavery in Egypt through Moses, and Moses was the one through whom God gave His people the Law. But now One greater than Moses was here (see Deuteronomy 34:12). In the Old Testament, one of the greatest honors God gave to a person was to call them "my servant." But here God speaks directly from heaven, saying, "This is my Son, whom I love." The Son of God is far greater than a servant.

Moses and Elijah were not in competition with Jesus. There was no jealousy. They must have been thrilled to meet Him. Jesus was the entire reason for the ministries Moses and Elijah carried. The Law (represented by Moses) and the Prophets (represented by Elijah) all pointed to Jesus.

Jesus is the same yesterday, today, and forevermore, but He is translated to us differently as we dive into the deep seas of revelation and discover who He is. We will see the fullness of who He is in glory, where we will experience our own transfiguration. Who are others seeing us as? The three saw Him and heard Him introduced as the Son of God. Are we abiding in Him so that others see Christ through our lives being glorified through Him?

The three disciples—Peter, James, and John—had their lives forever changed because they saw Jesus as He is. What would our lives look like if we saw Jesus as He is? What would our living look like? Our sight would open to another level of belief, and we would be able to accomplish more because of our level of trust.

Our belief system is faulty at times. This is what keeps us from walking in abundant life. When we continue to live from a defeated place, we receive limited results. Life becomes limited when it is not lived from a place of revelation. When Jesus is revealed, the discovery of life begins, and we learn that there is more to life than what has been.

Revelation stops when we stop believing. I believe what I do not yet see. I'm living a revealed life, and it is unfolding day by day. But often we do not see the signs—the things God is showing to transport us from one place to another. The importance of any matter is gauged by moments in time. When we focus long enough, the flow will come, and we learn how to move in the flow of life.

Revelation never stops flowing, but there are moments when it becomes more frequent. It depends on your abiding in Him, your seeking after Him, your embrace of who He is, and your submission to His timing.

CHAPTER 10
LIFE IN GOD'S GARDEN

The earth is waiting for man's authorization to cause things to come into existence.

"Then God said, let the earth bring forth the living creature, according to its kind: cattle and creeping thing, and the beast of the earth, each, according to his kind, and it was so."

— GENESIS 1:24

"For the earnest expectation of the creature waiteth for the manifestation of the sons of God.
For we know that the whole creation groaneth and travaileth in pain together until now."

— ROMANS 8:19;22

"The earth is the Lord's, and the fulness thereof; the world, and they that dwell therein.

> *For he hath founded it upon the seas, and established it upon the floods."*
>
> — PSALM 24:1-2

A "land," such as the "land of Israel," had defined borders, and all of the "lands" were pieced together much like a shattered piece of pottery that has been glued back together. It is interesting to note that the English word "earth" appears to be closely related to the Hebrew word *erets*. We were taken from the dust of the earth, and the earth gave birth to man by God's hand.

> *"Let the peoples praise You, O God; Let all the peoples praise You. Then the earth shall yield her increase; God, our own God, shall bless us."*
>
> — PSALM 67:5-6

> *"The Lord God formed man from the dust of the earth. He blew into his nostrils the breath of life, and man became a living being. Greek: And God formed dust from the earth into a man and he blew into his face a breath of life, and the man became a living soul."*
>
> — GENESIS 2:7

Dust is made of fine particles of solid matter. On earth, it generally consists of particles lifted into the atmosphere from various sources, such as soil carried by the wind.

So, when the wind of God was blowing, it formed the dust from the earth. These were fine particles of dirt, but the real substance of man came when God breathed into him. Dust cannot exist without wind, and in the same way, when God spoke, His breath moved and the wind blew.

Now consider this: What happens when we speak? The very definition of dust reminds us that its particles are suspended in the atmosphere. Likewise, the wind and breath of God are ready to form what we release with our words. God Himself is the wind, and wind represents movement.

Everything was already set in place for man to thrive, and all of it came from the earth. But nothing grows or flourishes without seed, nutrients, and movement.

The word *wind* comes from the sense "to move, to flow, to rush, or to drive along." It is air in motion with any degree of velocity. When the air moves gently, we call it a breeze. With greater strength, we call it a fresh wind. When it blows violently, we call it a gale, a storm, or a tempest. Winds are even identified by the compass point from which they blow—the north wind, the east wind, the south wind, the west wind, and so on.

In the same way, the wind of God takes your words where they need to go. Do you realize that your prayers travel faster than the fastest form of human travel—even faster than a rocket? When we pray according to God's will, we literally bring heaven to earth. Walking in God's will is the activation of the prayer; it is the forming of God's Word coming to life. God breathes on every word and every promise. This is why, when a prophetic word is spoken, two things happen:

1. Everything that doesn't line up with the Word of action gets exposed and removed if we yield to this process.
2. Everything starts coming into place to form the promise, but the old has to be exposed first and removed.

This is the divine transfer—take this old life and give me my new life. It is old because it has served its purpose; it has been used and expressed to its full capacity. Wind is the perceptible natural movement of the air, especially in the form of a current of air blowing from a particular direction. When storms come in our lives, it is the violent wind that we have the power to speak to and command to be calm.

We have the power to endure the storm because the wind is forming something. Something is being produced by the wind—by the violent wind—and when the dust settles, out of the dust comes the promise. You don't see it in the storm. Some storms are purposeful. Adam didn't know he was formed until the breath of God blew into him, and what was formed was able to live and thrive.

That's why God said that He doesn't want the church having only the form. The form is empty, with no substance. The form has no life until you tell the wind where to go with your words. Your words direct the wind; the dust can't move, the particles can't move, until they know what to do. How do they know what to do? When we speak the Word. God's creation is in tune with His divine plan. The earth is waiting for us to speak the right thing. When you move, you release something into the atmosphere, but when you connect movement with speech, it is like a whirlwind—everything you speak is caught up in the wind, and the wind takes the words where they need to go.

Dancing is a form of worship and a form of releasing the purposes of God into the atmosphere. A dancer moves with the song that is being played, and the wind of God releases what needs to be released to those in the geographical area and in the heavens as well. The earth is positioned to yield to what you say, which is what the Lord says.

His Word alone is powerful.

> *"For the word of God is living and active, sharper than any two-edged sword, piercing to the division of soul and of spirit, of joints and of marrow, and discerning the thoughts and intentions of the heart."*
>
> — HEBREWS 4:12

The Word of God lives, meaning anything that has life will not remain still. It is active—engaging, ready to engage, operating, working, functioning, effective, diligent, and committed.

A two-edged sword is a situation or course of action having both positive and negative effects. Two-edged swords have been around as long as swords themselves. A sword whose blade is sharpened on both sides is able to penetrate and cut at every contact point and with every movement. This means it can be thrust more quickly and deeply and can cut more easily.

A two-edged sword penetrates. Through the Spirit, God reveals things "to our spirits precisely as though we had no bodies at all" (*Teachings of Presidents of the Church: Joseph Smith* [2007], 475). His Word can cut through culture, habits, biases, preconceptions, and doubts to speak to the innermost part of us, whether we are righteous or wicked.

The blood plays a role in temperature regulation. It distributes heat throughout the body, from the core to the surface and vice versa. By changing the blood flow to the skin, the body can control heat exchange at its surface with its surroundings. Your body has exothermic chemical reactions occurring in various organs. A by-product of those chemical reactions is heat, which is given off, and the blood absorbs that heat and redistributes it among the organs. This evens out the spread of heat and ensures that the entire body remains at a consistent temperature.

> *Thus the heavens and the earth were finished, and all the host of them.*
> *And on the seventh day God ended his work which he had made; and he rested on the seventh day from all his work which he had made.*
> *And God blessed the seventh day, and sanctified it: because that in it he had rested from all his work which God created and made.*
> *These are the generations of the heavens and of the earth when they were created, in the day that the Lord God made the earth and the heavens,*

> *And every plant of the field before it was in the earth, and every herb of the field before it grew: for the Lord God had not caused it to rain upon the earth, and there was not a man to till the ground.*
>
> — GENESIS 2:1-5

The heavens and the earth were formed, but they were empty. The earth would serve no purpose if we were not here. Without people, there would be no need for vegetation, animals, business, ministries, government, and so much more. While God created the earth in sequence, He always had mankind in mind. Everything He made was for us to enjoy. He laid the foundation for us first.

It is like a pregnant woman preparing for birth—she makes ready in advance for the child she knows is coming. In the same way, God prepared for our arrival. We must also prepare for the season we are embarking upon right now.

- *Proper nourishment:* "And every plant of the field before it was in the earth, and every herb of the field before it grew" (Genesis 2:5). God made it before it was planted. In the same way, He made you before you were conceived in your mother's womb.

- *A place to live:* "Thus the heavens and the earth were finished, and all the host of them" (Genesis 2:1). God provided a dwelling place for us.

- *Clothing to wear:* "And they were both naked, the man and his wife, and were not ashamed" (Genesis 2:25). Yet later, God clothed His people in righteousness: "Let Your priests be clothed with righteousness, and let Your saints shout for joy" (Psalm 132:9).

- *Checking in with the doctor:* Just as expectant parents check in with their physician, Adam and Eve walked with God in the cool of the day (Genesis 3:8). God had already given them instructions on what to do and what not to do in the garden.

The second part of Genesis 2:5 says,

> *"For the LORD God had not caused it to rain upon the earth, and there was not a man to till the ground."*
>
> — GENESIS 2:5

He made every plant of the field before it was in the earth. Do you realize that the resolution to everything in your life is already formed? It is formed before it is released. It is formed before your arrival into the next season of obedience to God.

Not being in place will stop the rain from being released in the earth. God did not release the vegetation or the rain to cause it to grow because man was not yet here to tend to it.

So, my question to you today is this: Are you ready to tend, nurture, and value what God wants to pour out before the pouring takes place? Prepare for the pour. Make room for the pour.

Elijah told the widow woman to gather empty vessels so the oil could be poured out (2 Kings 4:3–6). She even went to her neighbors to collect more. This shows us the importance of being open to help. We cannot fulfill our assignments alone. What others carry will help you carry what God has placed upon you.

We are the Body of Christ, and Jesus is the Head.

> "Christ is also the head of the church, which is his body. He is the beginning, supreme over all who rise from the dead. So he is first in everything."
>
> — COLOSSIANS 1:18

> *"But there went up a mist from the earth, and watered the whole face of the ground.*
> *And the Lord God formed man of the dust of the ground, and breathed into his nostrils the breath of life; and man became a living soul."*
>
> — GENESIS 2:6

Man came forward after the rain fell upon the earth. Think about what happens when dirt is watered—it turns into mud, into clay. The Word tells us that we are the clay and God is the Potter. The ground must be moist in order for a seed to receive the proper nutrients and grow. The earth is like the wheel, spinning in orbit. Time turns, seasons change, and in that turning the making happens. A potter cannot form pottery unless the wheel is turning. So there has to be movement. You cannot stay still and expect to produce. We are connected to the Vine. We carry seeds that must be watered, and we also have seeds to sow into others.

> *"And the LORD God planted a garden eastward in Eden; and there He put the man whom He had formed. And out of the ground the LORD God made every tree grow that is pleasant to the sight and good for food; the tree of life also in the midst of the garden, and the tree of knowledge of good and evil."*
>
> — GENESIS 2:8-9

God is true to His Word. Pray His Word. When you do your part, you partner with heaven. When you posture yourself, God moves. Do you think that if Adam and Eve had known their choice would affect generations after them, they would have made the same choice? Do you realize that the choices you make today will affect generations after you?

We must learn how to prepare for this season, understanding the times we are in and positioning ourselves for what God is doing. To truly know God's original plan for our lives, we must return to the beginning, where His intent and design were first revealed. In doing so, we gain strategies that not only prepare us for today but also equip us for the years to come.

The Book of Genesis opens with:

- The formation of the solar system
- The preparation of land for habitation
- The creation of life on earth
- All eight acts of creation accomplished in six days

Sometimes God has to take us back to the beginning—back to the originality of things—to remind us of why we are here and of His promises.

> "In the beginning was the Word, and the Word was with God, and the Word was God."
>
> — JOHN 1:1

Genesis is full of beginnings:

1. The Godhead was introduced and established.
2. The world was created—the heavens, earth, and life within.
3. The fall of man brought sin into the earth.
4. The flood came.
5. Pregnancy and childbirth began.
6. Murder entered through Cain and Abel.

Back to Eden means returning to a place of purity and obedience before the fall. Adam and Eve fell from an elevated place. God protected them until they breached His covenant. Eden was paradise—a garden built by God as the home for Adam and Eve. It was a state of innocence, perfect happiness, and divine pleasure. Eden does not have to be a physical place—it can be a spiritual state of being or a mindset. We are spirit beings, and our spirit must be filled with the Spirit of God to live in the supernatural. The Holy Spirit is what makes you supernatural.

God placed man in the garden to tend and keep it. He created the garden first, filled it, and then placed man there. In the same way, you were sent here to tend, cultivate, and steward what is already in place. Jesus came to die for the world that was already formed and created. John the Baptist came as His forerunner. Moses came to lead Israel out of Egypt's bondage, and Joshua carried the assignment further when Moses could not enter the Promised Land. And so on. Each path was already prepared. When we realize that the provision and purpose have already been made, we understand that we are not here by chance. This is not random; it is an organized, established kingdom that we are heirs of.

God made man in His likeness and image.

- *Likeness* means resemblance, appearance, and spiritual attributes that reflect God's moral qualities.

- God gave us dominion because He Himself has dominion. He rules and subdues. He said, "I've done it in eternity; now I want to manifest that same power in the earth." He commanded us to be fruitful, multiply, and replenish.

The ability to sustain and rule rests in continued obedience to God's role as King of all. God saw everything He made and declared it good. He is good; therefore, everything He creates is good.

> "And the LORD God formed man of the dust of the ground, and breathed into his nostrils the breath of life; and man became a living being."

— GENESIS 2:7

After God planted the garden, He put Adam there. Out of the ground He caused every tree to grow that was pleasant and good for food. This reveals the intentional care of a Father who prepares everything His creation will need before placing him in his assignment. God did not create Adam first and then scramble to provide resources; instead, He established the environment, the nourishment, the beauty, and the provision beforehand. Adam opened his eyes to a world already flourishing—a world fully equipped to sustain the purpose God placed within him.

Provision and pleasure existed side by side. The trees were not only for survival, but also for delight. God designed the garden to appeal to Adam's senses, to engage his mind, and to stir his spirit. God wanted Adam to live in a setting where His goodness could be seen, tasted, experienced, and enjoyed. Every tree testified of God's generosity. Every fruit reflected His abundance. The garden was a picture of God's heart—a place where man would never have to question whether God was willing to care for him.

Provision preceded purpose. God prepared the environment first, then placed Adam into the work of stewarding it. Before Adam was given responsibility, he was surrounded by evidence of God's faithfulness. Before he was asked to rule, he was immersed in the goodness of God's creation. Adam's assignment was never meant to be carried out from a place of lack, but from a place of fullness and divine supply.

> *"The LORD God planted a garden eastward in Eden, and there He put the man whom He had formed. And out of the ground the LORD God made every tree grow that is pleasant to the sight and good for food. The tree of life was also in the midst of the garden, and the tree of the knowledge of good and evil."*
>
> — GENESIS 2:8–9

CRYSTAL LOVE

> *"Then the LORD God took the man and put him in the garden of Eden to tend and keep it. And the LORD God commanded the man, saying, 'Of every tree of the garden you may freely eat; but of the tree of the knowledge of good and evil you shall not eat, for in the day that you eat of it you shall surely die.'"*
>
> — GENESIS 2:15–17

The garden was Adam's altar—a sacred place to be maintained. Will you be the altar? Will you be the garden? When we yield to God, He sets us in a place of abundance—a secret place of favor. Regardless of what is happening around us, we will prosper spiritually and naturally. The garden represents that sacred place where only you and God commune. It is the place of His presence, His dwelling, His shelter.

> *"He who dwells in the secret place of the Most High shall abide under the shadow of the Almighty."*
>
> — PSALM 91:1

- To *dwell* means to live, to reside.
- To *abide* means to remain permanently, to make it your lifelong residence.
- To *abide under His shadow* means to live under His shelter, covering, and protection.

This is what Eden was for Adam and Eve—a place of covering and protection. Adam was placed there to care for the garden before Eve arrived, and then Eve was given to assist him. God specified two trees: the Tree of Life and the Tree of the Knowledge of Good and Evil. This was the place of choice—the place of *obedience* or *disobedience*. A river flowed through Eden and parted into four riverheads to water the garden. In the same way, God not only gives you abundance, but He also gives you the grace to maintain what He releases to you.

God told man to tend and keep the garden.

- *Tend* means to cultivate, to work regularly, to nurture.
- *Keep* means to maintain, to guard, to protect, to continue in a specific condition.

Adam did not have to search for God. God was right there with him.

> *"Ask, and it shall be given to you; seek, and you shall find; knock, and it shall be opened unto you."*
>
> — MATTHEW 7:7

> *And the Lord God said, "It is not good that man should be alone; I will make him a helper comparable to him." Out of the ground the Lord God formed every beast of the field and every bird of the air, and brought them to Adam to see what he would call them. And whatever Adam called each living creature, that was its name. So Adam gave names to all cattle, to the birds of the air, and to every beast of the field. But for Adam there was not found a helper comparable to him.*
>
> *And the Lord God caused a deep sleep to fall on Adam, and he slept; and He took one of his ribs, and closed up the flesh in its place. Then the rib which the Lord God had taken from man He made into a woman, and He brought her to the man.*
>
> *And Adam said: 'This is now bone of my bones*
> *And flesh of my flesh;*
> *She shall be called Woman,*

Because she was taken out of Man.'

*Therefore a man shall leave his father and mother and be
    joined to his wife, and they shall become one flesh.
And they were both naked, the man and his wife, and were not
    ashamed.*

— GENESIS 2:18-25

CHAPTER 11
REVELATION & RELATIONSHIP

The Holy Spirit is a person you should become very well acquainted with. I want you to take a moment and think about what I'm saying. You have a supernatural Being living on the inside of you as part of you. This Person helps you with your life. Oftentimes, we pick up our telephones to Google certain things and do research. But imagine having someone living inside your body who has the answer to all things. If this is true, then don't you think this is someone you should really get to know?

I think out of all the relationships you've embraced and entertained, and out of all the conversations in your life, the Holy Spirit should be valued greatly. It is nothing like having a destination but not being sure how to get there. Whether you are driving, walking, catching a train, or even flying a plane, you have to know where you're going—or even if you're going anywhere at all. One thing I can assure you is that in life, there is always a destination to arrive at. There is nobody living on this earth who can stay in one place forever.

Now let's talk about the physical. Since you cannot sit in one place and never move—if you do, this will cause not only spiritual death but also physical death. I have heard many stories of people who worked jobs for twenty to thirty years or more, and as soon as they retired, their health began to decline. It is sad to hear that many lost their lives. Some died of natural causes, and some fell sick—all because they stopped moving. Staying in one place all the time can stop everything from flowing in your life.

People think that only older individuals develop certain illnesses. But if you do not take care of your physical body and allow God to give you the blueprint for how to keep your temple intact, then it will fall apart and you will age quickly. God preserves our soul and will preserve our soul until the day of redemption, but we must also help in maintaining the things that we do have control over. For example, we have control over what time we go to bed, who we are in relationships with, the jobs we take, the food we eat, whether we exercise, and whether we take proper steps with good hygiene.

Everything in our lives, if not given the proper attention, has the potential to take us on a journey that God did not map out for us. You could have every area of your life out of sync with God's order and watch everything turn into total chaos because there is no order. But if God is in control of every area of our lives—our physical well-being, our emotions, our social areas, and our spiritual lives—then the enemy has no foothold in our souls. We can walk in total alignment with God's perfect will for our lives, and everything will flow as He has ordained.

This does not mean that our lives will be free from trouble, but it does mean that whenever anything comes, it will not and cannot pull us out of the perfect will of God. So here we are, on this journey with God in a world filled with distractions, yet we have the tools to counteract whatever tries to take our attention away from our divine assignment.

Though we have a broken, fallen nature because of the fall of man —born in sin and shaped in iniquity—that does not have to be our chosen path. God sent His Son in the flesh, which was Himself, into the world to show us what we are really fighting against. He came to show us how to fight with both the divine and the natural man and to be effective. He also reminded us that we are not fighting in our own abilities—it is in God's abilities.

This can only be seen and understood in the spirit realm through the eyes of God. The reason it remains a mystery is because unless you seek it out, you will not understand it. God will not minimize who He is to suit our carnality—we must come up higher to understand. God says, "Let Me show you what you have. Let Me show you what you have access to. Let Me show you what I meant when I said I would give you the keys to the Kingdom."

That means that everything locked up is not for everybody. The only people who can access what God has are the people with the keys. When Jesus asked the disciples, "Who do men say that I am?" they each gave their answer. But when He asked His disciples—the ones who had been following Him all along—"Who do you say that I am?" Peter rose up and said, "You are the Christ, the Son of the living God."

It is only upon our revelation of who God is that we are able to build. Right after that, Jesus said, "Flesh and blood has not revealed this to you." Revelation comes only from the Spirit of God. In the spirit realm, Peter unknowingly tapped into a revelation of who God was and is because of his hunger. And since God is the same yesterday, today, and forever, He never changes. Seasons change, times change, but God's will for our lives never changes. Who He is never changes—He is eternal.

The keys are the revelation: to know who He is, to know who we are, and to know what we have to fight against whatever tries to stop us from walking in our true purpose.

> *"When Jesus came to the region of Caesarea Philippi, he asked his disciples, "Who do people say the Son of Man is?" And they said, 'Some say that thou art John the Baptist: some, Elias; and others, Jeremias, or one of the prophets.' He saith unto them, 'But whom say ye that I am? And Simon Peter answered and said, 'Thou art the Christ, the Son of the living God.'*

> *And Jesus answered and said unto him, 'Blessed art thou, Simon Bar-jona: for flesh and blood hath not revealed it unto thee, but my Father which is in heaven.*
> *And I say also unto thee, That thou art Peter, and upon this rock I will build my church; and the, gates of hell shall not prevail against it.*
> *And I will give unto thee the keys of the kingdom of heaven: and whatsoever thou shalt bind on earth shall be bound in heaven: and whatsoever thou shalt loose on earth shall be loosed in heaven.*
>
> — MATTHEW 16:13-19

The Lord taught that His Church was to be built on the rock of revelation—divine truths revealed by God Himself—and that Christ is the Son of the living God; therefore, the gates of hell shall not prevail against His Church.

The keys of the Kingdom were promised to Peter, and he exercised that authority as he associated with the other members of the Twelve and presided over them.

There were a number of occasions when the Savior took only Peter, James, and John with Him, undoubtedly for additional spiritual experiences and instruction. When Jesus went up into the Mount of Transfiguration to prepare for His coming ordeal, He took these three Apostles with Him so that, having seen His glory—the glory of the Only Begotten of the Father—their hearts would be fortified and their faith strengthened as they gazed upon this heavenly event. There they received the promised keys of the priesthood. During this divine moment, Moses and Elias also appeared, and the three Apostles heard the voice of the Father bearing witness that Jesus is His Beloved Son and commanding them to hear and obey Him.

From the glory revealed at the Mount of Transfiguration, we are drawn back to the very beginning, when God separated light from darkness and set His order in motion. In that unfolding plan of redemption, He later chose Abraham, through whom all the families of the earth would be blessed.

Abraham left Haran to go to Canaan, the promised land. He went with the plan of God and arrived at the place God had ordained. The land was already his; it had already been promised to God's people, so it was not meant for him alone. When they arrived in Canaan, God promised to give it to his descendants, and Abraham built altars to the Lord. You become who God intends you to be so that others can come into a place of obedience to God.

> *Lord, I build an altar here. I agree with Your plan, I say yes to Your plan, and I prepare to execute Your plan. An altar is never just a structure—it is a place of sacrifice, worship, prayer, dedication, commitment, and covenant. Every time we build an altar in our lives, it marks a decisive moment where we align ourselves fully with God's will and commit to walk in His purpose.*

Isaac's journey from the Valley of Gerar to Beersheba came after a season of prosperity and conflict with the Philistines. His blessings had grown so evident that Abimelech, the king of the Philistines, asked him to leave because he had become too powerful. Imagine Isaac thinking, "I'm too powerful to expand here, and this is not even the fullness of what God has for me—yet my enemy is pushing me out." Sometimes being forced out is not rejection but redirection into greater territory.

Isaac prospered even in the valley, but imagine what awaited him at the peak of where God was taking him. Before leaving, he dug up the wells that had been stopped by the Philistines, reclaiming the inheritance of his father Abraham. These wells represented more than water—they were symbols of blessing, life, and divine appointment. Genesis 26:17–18 records that Isaac settled in the valley, reopened the wells, and called them by the same names his father had given.

Wells in Scripture often mark moments of destiny: Hagar found refreshment and hope by a well in her despair; Moses met Zipporah at a well in Midian, stepping into forty years of preparation; and

Isaac's own servant encountered Rebekah at a well, securing God's promise for the next generation. Wells are not only about provision but about divine setups—strategic alignments where God reveals purpose, supplies needs, and forges relationships.

In the same way, God is reopening wells within us that have been stopped up by disappointment, curses, mental battles, or spiritual stagnation. Jesus said in John 4:14,

> *"The water I give will become in them a spring of water welling up to eternal life."*
>
> — JOHN 4:14

That well is not man-made—it is the work of the Holy Spirit. You cannot produce it, but you can call it forth: "I speak to the well within me. I command the treasure inside of me to come forth."

Water in Scripture represents the Spirit, deliverance, provision, judgment, cleansing, and new beginnings. Isaac's servants, in obedience, dug and discovered not just ordinary wells but a spring-fed well —a direct, natural source of flowing water (Genesis 26:19). Likewise, God is calling us to tap into the direct source, not a secondhand flow. This next dimension is coming from within—from communion with Him. It is a new level that cannot be measured by the old, because everything about it is different.

Just as Elisha received a double portion after Elijah was carried away in a chariot of fire, so too are we called into new realms of revelation, power, and purity. God consumes the old, closes out the past, and releases mantles for the future. For Elisha, the fire purified the path so that he would not repeat Elijah's mistakes, and the wind of God propelled him forward. In the same way, God's Word lifts us into altitude—into higher places where we see with distance and clarity.

But elevation requires endurance. Just as runners train to expand their lungs, we too must be trained by trials, disappointments, and pruning so that when pressure comes, it only sharpens us. Isaac would not have discovered new wells had he not been pushed out. Sometimes God allows opposition to reposition us, because left in comfort, we would never move.

In the same way that Jesus was transfigured before His disciples, revealing the glory of God, there comes a time when God announces the closing of one season and the birthing of another. These transitions take us from one dimension to the next—not by effort but by revelation of who Jesus Christ is. Without revelation, we risk living beneath our calling, missing divine appointments, and treating destiny casually. But when the Spirit opens our eyes, He unstops the wells within and fills us with fresh hunger for more of Him.

As Paul declared in Ephesians 3, mysteries are revealed by the Spirit, strengthening the inner man and unveiling the riches of Christ. With the keys of the Kingdom in our hands, we move in authority, identity, and dominion. The Spirit of the Lord—the fullness of His manifold wisdom—anchors us in love and fills us with the fullness of God. This is the springing well that flows from revelation, producing transformation and releasing us into dimensions of glory to glory.

Isaac knew this truth when he named the wells the same names as Abraham, securing continuity of blessing. Generations later, his son Jacob would return to Beersheba, worship there, and encounter God again—proving that what God establishes in one generation flows as a wellspring into the next.

There are some signs that indicate the presence of the Holy Spirit:

1. A changed life: The Holy Spirit transforms a person's heart and character, leading to a noticeable change in behavior and attitude.

2. Fruit of the Spirit: The Holy Spirit produces love, joy, peace, patience, kindness, goodness, faithfulness, gentleness, and self-control in a person's life.

3. Spiritual gifts: The Holy Spirit gives believers supernatural abilities to serve God and others, such as prophecy, healing, speaking in tongues, and wisdom.

4. Conviction of sin: The Holy Spirit brings awareness of sin and the need for repentance in a person's life.

5. Prayer and worship: The Holy Spirit enables believers to pray and worship God in spirit and truth, with a deep sense of intimacy and connection.

6. Guidance and discernment: The Holy Spirit guides believers in making wise decisions and discerning God's will for their lives.

7. Unity and community: The Holy Spirit unites believers in Christ, creating a sense of community and fellowship that transcends cultural, racial, and social barriers.

INTERVIEW WITH THE HOLY SPIRIT

It is important to pause and reflect on the One who makes all revelation possible—the Holy Spirit. He is not a distant force but a present Helper, Teacher, and Guide. He brings clarity where there is confusion, truth where there are questions, and revelation where there is hunger. When we inquire of Him, He responds with wisdom that aligns our lives with the heart of God.

1. Why does sin have a generational impact?

The generational impact of sin can be traced back to Adam and Eve's disobedience in the Garden of Eden, which resulted in the introduction of sin and death into the world and the corruption of mankind. Romans 5:12 says,

> *"Therefore, just as sin entered the world through one man, and death through sin, and in this way death came to all people because all sinned."*

We see this generationally in our personal lives, in our families, among friends and loved ones, and throughout the world. Humanity has been heavily impacted by the repercussions of walking in and yielding to the sinful nature into which we were born.

2. Why were humans created so differently from everything else made in creation?

Genesis 1:27 states,

> *"So God created mankind in His own image, in the image of God He created them; male and female He created them."*

Humans were created differently from everything else in creation because they were made in the image of God. This means that humans have a spiritual dimension and the ability to think, reason, and make choices according to the Spirit of God. Humans cannot be compared to any other creature in creation because God purposely designed it that way.

3. Why are words so powerful?

Words are powerful because God created the world through speech. Genesis 1:3 says,

> *"And God said, 'Let there be light,' and there was light."*

Proverbs 18:21 says,

> *"The tongue has the power of life and death, and those who love it will eat its fruit."*

Words have the power to build up or tear down, encourage or discourage, and convey truth or lies.

4. Is there a way to enhance our memory retention?

The Bible offers insight on improving memory retention through practices such as repetition and meditation. Joshua 1:8 says,

> *"Keep this Book of the Law always on your lips; meditate on it day and night, so that you may be careful to do everything written in it. Then you will be prosperous and successful."*

Proverbs 7:3 instructs,

> *"Bind them on your fingers; write them on the tablet of your heart."*

5. What does Heaven look and feel like?

The Bible provides glimpses of what Heaven will be like but acknowledges that our understanding is limited by our human experience. Revelation 21:4 describes a place where there is no more death, mourning, crying, or pain. First Corinthians 2:9 states,

> *"No eye has seen, no ear has heard, no mind has conceived what God has prepared for those who love Him."*

6. What does eternity feel like?

The Word of God lets us know that our understanding of eternity is limited. Revelation 22:5 says,

> *"There will be no more night. They will not need the light of a lamp or the light of the sun, for the Lord God will give them light. And they will reign for ever and ever."*

We know that eternity will be characterized by closeness to God and an absence of sin, pain, and death. Just as eternity reveals the fullness of God's presence beyond time, creation reflects His power within time—when He spoke, even the earth responded with life.

CHAPTER 12
CHOSEN TO LIVE IN TWO WORLDS

You were selected to live in two worlds—to fulfill one purpose. There is a divine tension that exists in the life of every believer: we are called to live in two realms at once. One is the spiritual—the Kingdom of Heaven—and the other is the natural—the earth we walk daily. This is not a curse but a calling—a divine appointment. You were born into the earth but predestined from Heaven. You were created in time but chosen in eternity.

This reality gives meaning to everything we face. It explains the groanings within us, the ache in the atmosphere, and the yearning for order amidst chaos. We were there from the beginning in the mind of God: God the Father, Jesus the Son, and the Holy Spirit. There is nothing new under the sun. What we have inside of us was present at creation. We were not a Plan B, but part of the original plan when God created the heavens and the earth.

We are earth in human form; we come from the dust of the ground and were breathed into by God—which is the Spirit of God—while the blood of Jesus stands as the redemptive protocol connecting us to the divine. God is Alpha and Omega, the beginning and the end, the first and the last. All of His plan was in Him, completed and imparted into us through His Ruach—His breath, His Spirit—that has been active before and from the beginning of time, a Spirit with no start and no finish.

The kairos of time helps us understand that we were not an aftermath of the fall of Satan—Lucifer, the son of the morning (2 Corinthians 11:14; Isaiah).

When we understand foundational truths about how and why things were, how they came to be, and their eternal significance, it becomes difficult to conform to a misjudged form of godliness or to the powerless commands of the kingdom of darkness. It is the ultimate betrayal of the devil to try to convince us that we are not valuable or qualified to confront his usurped authority. He has attempted to force his way into our lives—into our sacred places that hold the capacity to transform lives and nations.

We cannot continue to sell our birthrights and blessings because of the manipulative, continuous dialogue in the mind that has sought to deceive us all the way from the Garden of Intimacy—from the beginning until now. The Word of God in Matthew says,

> *"For then there will be great tribulation, such as has not been from the beginning of the world until now, no, and never will be. And if those days had not been cut short, no human being would be saved. But for the sake of the elect those days will be cut short."*
>
> — MATTHEW 24:21-22

Though the exchange began at the beginning of time, no one could have imagined the trickle-down effect that one experience would have on humanity. Yet God had a plan to save us from the great tribulation and the manifestation of evil. This is God's time; the devastation already exists. The kingdom of darkness has its time in the earthly realm, but it is already powerless against the Kingdom of Heaven in the spirit. And when you use this power to immobilize its abilities—in unity and strength—the Body of Christ, even though we may never meet in person, remains connected in spirit.

God speaks the same message across different time zones and seasons. This is why you may hear many people seemingly aligned, releasing what God desires in unison at a particular time: there is power in unity. More can be accomplished in a shorter time when many work together on the same agenda.

Romans 8:19-23 describes this longing clearly:

> *"For all creation is waiting eagerly for that future day when God will reveal who His children really are. The creation looks forward to the day when it will join God's children in glorious freedom from death and decay..."*
>
> — ROMANS 8:19-23

Creation is moaning because it is waiting on you—not just the you who punches the clock and pays bills, but the you who carries the DNA of God. To understand the functionality of having the DNA of God is to know what He sent you here to do and to fulfill it to full capacity—the one predestined to be holy and blameless before time began (Ephesians 1:3-5). You were not born into confusion; you were born into a calling.

The DNA of dominion is the full establishment of the Kingdom of Heaven in the earth realm. When God breathed life into man, it was not merely oxygen—it was identity. It was the deposit of Heaven's culture into earthly form. We are more than flesh and bone; we are Spirit-breathed, divine seeds placed in earthly soil to bear eternal fruit.

What are we filling the earth with? Have you satisfied the moan in the earth? God said, "Let them have dominion..." That is not just a suggestion; it is a kingdom decree. Dominion is not domination —it is divine order. It is putting things back into their proper alignment under the rulership of Christ. Yet we cannot fully rule in the earth unless we first learn how to live from the spirit. This is why the Holy Spirit is essential. He is not a bonus to your faith— He is the very breath that makes faith possible. It is by the Spirit that we receive revelation of who we are and what we are here to do.

Romans 8:20–23 (NLT) says,

> "Against its will, all creation was subjected to God's curse. But with eager hope...For we know that the whole creation has been groaning together in the pains of childbirth until now. And we believers also groan, even though we have the Holy Spirit within us as a foretaste of future glory, for we long for our bodies to be released from sin and suffering. We, too, wait with eager hope for the day when God will give us our full rights as his adopted children, including the new bodies he has promised us."

It was not our will, but the earth's will; the earth was not created to be cursed. The earth was not meant to exist in a crippled position. It was pure and free from fault—a magnificent masterpiece made for humanity to dominate and to enjoy the pleasures of the Kingdom of God. The Kingdom—the government of God—has no flaws or blemishes.

When man sinned, he lost intimate citizenship. Being licensed to sin is not true freedom; citizenship means freedom *from* sin, not freedom *in* unrighteousness. Obedience opens the door to the amenities and abilities of your Kingdom citizenship, determining your Kingdom status.

God prophesied man's assignment before the fight. There was an anointing and proclamation over man before the trial. This is why He said, "The day you hear My voice, harden not your heart." This voice is distinctive from any other because it prompts the heart toward covenant, not control. A covenant requires agreement. God can reacquaint us with the agreement established before our birth through our parents.

Agreement means obedience: "How can two walk together unless they agree?" We walk with God in the cool of the day. In the garden of life, a flow of release and transfer occurs. God releases and transfers to us as His children, and we reproduce after our kind, just as all creation does. The Kingdom of God produces after its kind.

Genesis 1:11–12 says,

> "God made the beasts of the earth after their kind, and the cattle after their kind, and everything that creeps on the ground after its kind; and God saw that it was good. The earth brought forth vegetation, plants yielding seed after their kind, and trees bearing fruit with seed in them, after their kind; and God saw that it was good."

We are not all alike in appearance, but we are alike in one common goal and connection. We carry the DNA of God, which makes us brothers and sisters in Christ, sharing the same assignment with different distinctions.

THE BLESSING AND BURDEN OF DUAL CITIZENSHIP

Living in two worlds is beautiful—but it is not always easy. There is sacrifice. There is struggle. There are seasons when your spirit is willing but your flesh is weak. There are moments when you feel the pressure of one world colliding with the demands of another.

The blessing—and the pitfall—of living in two worlds is that one can overpower the other in thought and deeds. The only problem with this scenario is that the two cannot become one. You are subject to one—the heavenly realm—yet you reign, rule, and govern in the other—the earthly realm—because of the power and authority you receive from the heavenly realm.

You are not crazy for feeling the weight. You are chosen. Chosen people feel deeply. The disciples were chosen—they had earthly obligations with a heavenly assignment. We must learn how to extract ourselves from this physical world, where we were born, and live from the spirit. When your purpose is revealed, it opens the spirit world within you. By this known fact, you are able to read the script of your life. A person will feel compelled to act it out through the guidance of the Holy Spirit, just as we see demonstrated in the acts of the apostles.

You are chosen to be the demonstration of God's power on the earth—to show the existence of God and to prove that He is real by living in your chosen state: the administration of God in the earth. We are to administrate, command direction, and walk in governmental leadership so that God can be revealed, and our dependence on Him releases His authority into the earth. The hardest part is that we often try to express Him in our own way, with our own methods.

We came from our parents naturally, but we came from God historically. We are an extension of Him, which is why we can identify with Him. He is eternal in our thinking, and this is why we carry history within us through the Holy Spirit. He is the Ancient of Days. Days are recorded for history and for our time. He was there at the beginning of days; He initiated the days. Days do not exist to an eternal God. He said, "One day is as a thousand years, and a thousand years as one day" (2 Peter 3:8).

We are on man's time and God's time— *chronos* and *kairos*. Sometimes this makes us feel off, as if we are spiritually jet-lagged. We are in transition, trying to stay in alignment with the Kingdom of Heaven while living and functioning here on earth as though we were in Heaven, because this is where we truly belong. We are to have a Kingdom mindset with an earthly existence.

My mind is in the Kingdom, but my body and its functions exist in another realm—the earthly realm. We can only identify with God when we are one with Him.

> *"But he who is joined to the Lord becomes one spirit with him."*
>
> — 1 CORINTHIANS 6:17

We carry DNA family traits from God and from our natural families. The blessing—and the burden—of this is that some traits from our earthly families must be dismissed so the DNA of God can be active and unhindered. You were chosen by God. Matthew, the tax collector, was chosen to record valuable information—to calculate what was paid, allocated, and owed. He had the gift to capture Jesus' life events in expressive detail. He was a gift from God to the world, appointed to express the life and ministry of Jesus.

He was chosen to do this. God handpicked us specifically for what we are to do. We were made for it; it is who we are. Nothing outside your purpose flows rightly. For the chosen, God does not allow comfort in disobedience. Some may feel discomfort and simply move on, but the chosen feel misery until they align with their purpose. Matthew was born at the perfect time to release who he was on the earth.

To know where you are going, you must know where you came from. Your origin plays a significant role in how you reach your destination. The DNA through the blood of His Son erases the earthly traits that hold us back. As we read in Scripture, Abel's blood cried out (Genesis 4:10). God confronted Cain after he murdered Abel, saying,

> *"The voice of your brother's blood cries out to Me from the ground."*
>
> — GENESIS 4:10

Abel's blood sought justice and vengeance. Our DNA may attempt to bind us to the earth, but the blood of Jesus cries louder. We cry out because spiritual attempts to assassinate our purpose seek to confine us to a realm where we can no longer live or function.

Romans 8:22–23 summarizes this:

> *"We believers also groan, even though we have the Holy Spirit within us as a foretaste of future glory, for we long for our bodies to be released from sin and suffering. We, too, wait with eager hope for the day when God will give us our full*

> *rights as his adopted children, including the new bodies he has promised us."*

There is a cry of relief as we anticipate future glory. Our bodies long for their glorified state. It is a cry of hope and expectation—for new, perfected bodies. We live out our future in hope of a better reality. We are not exempt from trials; in fact, we often face more because the enemy has studied our file in the courts of Heaven.

The courts of Heaven operate in order and truth. We have a Judge, a Mediator, an Accuser, and a record keeper. But here is the difference between a worldly courtroom and Heaven's: in Heaven, the Judge is also your Father. And your defense attorney? He already paid the price for your release.

> *"Who shall bring a charge against God's elect? It is God who justifies."*
>
> — ROMANS 3:33

Satan may accuse, but the blood still speaks. We plead our case before the Lord (1 Samuel 24:15). We petition God personally and globally as the Body of Christ. The case refers to the situation at hand. Without establishing a cause, it is difficult to hold anyone accountable. David cried out to God:

> *"May the Lord be our judge and decide between us. May he consider my cause and uphold it; may he vindicate me by delivering me from your hand."*
>
> — 1 SAMUEL 24:15

Saul had no reason to attack him multiple times.

> *"Plead my cause, O LORD, with those who strive with me; Fight against those who fight against me. Take hold of*

> *shield and buckler, and stand up for my help. Draw out the spear, and stop those who pursue me."*
>
> — PSALM 35:1–3

Without a cause, there is no case. God calls His children to judge righteously on earth. Judgment is restoration, not condemnation.

When we hear "judgment," we often envision wrath and fire. But God's judgment is restorative, rooted in righteousness. It seeks to rescue, not destroy.

In Hebrew, *Mishpat* means justice/judgment—to save, not destroy.

> *"He will judge the world in righteousness and the people in His faithfulness"*
>
> — PSALM 96:13

Psalm 96:10–11a, 13 says:

> *"Say among the nations, 'YHWH reigns; Indeed, the world is firmly established, it will not be moved. He will judge the peoples with equity.'"*

What have we done with the time God gave us? Have we walked in faith and accomplished His works? Have we judged each season properly, responding with clarity and wisdom? We must discern the times and move in sync with God.

> *"Let the heavens be glad, and let the earth rejoice... Be before YHWH, for He is coming; He is coming to judge the earth. He will judge the world in righteousness and the people in His faithfulness."*
>
> — PSALM 96:11-13

Notice that God's judgment is positive. It is not brimstone and fire. He judges with equity, righteousness, and faithfulness—to save the humble of the earth.

> *"Judge not according to appearance, but judge righteous judgment."*
>
> — JOHN 7:24

> *"The righteous will rejoice when they see the vengeance; He will wash his feet in the blood of the wicked. And men will say, 'Surely there is a reward for the righteous; Surely there is a God who judges on earth!'"*
>
> — PSALM 58:10–11

The prophetic book of Nahum outlines God's wrath and the destruction of Nineveh. Yet, interestingly, nowhere in Nahum is the word judgment or justice used. Why? Because God's judgment and wrath are separate. God's core is love, not hate. First and foremost, God uses judgment to seek out and reward those who love Him.

Psalm 76:8–9 says:

> *"You caused judgment to be heard from heaven; the earth feared and was still. God arose to judgment, to save all the humble of the earth."*

He uses judgment to save, not destroy—to save the meek who seek Him and love Him. Righteousness (*tsedeq*) is seeking God. In judgment, God finds those who long for a relationship with Him; He seeks the righteous.

Isaiah 30:18 says:

> *"Therefore YHWH longs to be gracious to you, and therefore*

> *He waits on high to have compassion on you. For YHWH is a God of justice; How blessed are all those who long for Him."*

But justice isn't for God alone. YHWH expects those who love Him to be advocates of justice on earth:

> *"Thus has YHWH of hosts said, 'Dispense true justice and practice kindness and compassion each to his brother; and do not oppress the widower, the orphan, the stranger or the poor; and do not devise evil in your hearts against one another.'"*
>
> — ZECHARIAH 7:9-10

> *"Learn to do good; Seek justice, Reprove the ruthless, Defend the orphan, Plead for the widow."*
>
> — ISAIAH 1:17

This kind of justice is an action WE are capable of doing, and what God expects us to do. What God does not want us to do is exact judgement. God alone is Judge.

> *"Humble yourselves before the Lord, and He will exalt you.*
> *Brothers, do not slander one another.*
> *Anyone who speaks against his brother or judges him speaks against the Law and judges it.*
> *And if you judge the Law, you are not a practitioner of the Law, but a judge of it.*
> *There is only one Lawgiver and Judge, the One who is able to save and destroy.*
> *But who are you to judge your neighbour?"*
>
> — JAMES 4:10-14

PLEADING HIS CAUSE & LIVING BETWEEN TWO WORLDS

That's why God calls us to plead His cause (Psalm 35). Judgment is not for revenge; it's for justice. Righteous judgment is Heaven's way of bringing order to earth. God uses it to find the humble, the willing, the obedient—and to align them with their original blueprint. That is why we must judge righteously, not by appearance (John 7:24).

When we live between two realms, we are called to be mediators—standing in the gap, discerning the times, and releasing the heart of God. The war between two worlds means that the Kingdom of Heaven has an obligation to fulfill in the earthly realm.

There are two frustrations:

1. We haven't been processed enough for where we are called to. The process, in simple terms, means an act of surrender, which automatically relinquishes your rights to your life.

2. We are flowing in something we aren't called to. God created the earth for us to rule and maintain, which is the assignment He has given us. Let's go back to the beginning to explain. He spoke light first because many of us are trying to live forward in darkness. We cannot expand the Kingdom of Heaven, release the illumination of Heavenly realms, or shine as the light of the world by building in darkness.

We must remember these three things:

1. *Build* – Jesus, the solid Rock
2. *Implement* – Tools and spiritual gifts
3. *Declare* – The intel from Heaven concerning what should be established in the earth

In other words: to build, we stand on Jesus, the solid Rock. To implement, we use the tools and spiritual gifts He has given us. And to declare, we release the intel from Heaven concerning what God intends to establish in the earth.

When the lights come on, the tools of implementation—the Holy Spirit, the gifts of the Spirit, and the nature of God—can activate. When we cannot see what we have, we cannot build what God said. When we cannot see, we cannot declare, because we do not know. A declaration is not something you make up—it is something God has already established. Heaven is on you, and divinity is fighting to be released, but the world system has many of us in a chokehold. The devil wants to shut us down.

We are not here to prove anything to anyone. We are living proof of God's promise, Jesus' redemptive power, and His saving grace. Many of us are not fighting the devil—we are fighting our purpose. We are fighting our divinity. It is the war inside of us.

John 16:33 says,

> *"I have told you these things, so that in Me you may have peace. In this world you will have trouble. But take heart! I have overcome the world."*

The world we are plugged into can distract us. If we are not careful, we will live more in this world than in Heaven. If we do not ascend, Heaven can never fully descend within us. Before Jesus could fulfill His purpose, He had to live in the earthly realm. His divinity was activated in baptism by John the Baptist and validated by the announcement of His coming.

What happens when you meet yourself? Some pitfalls occur because we have not fully met ourselves yet—we are living another life. Unless a seed dies and goes into the ground, it will not take root. Jesus died before He died. He died in baptism and in Gethsemane. The cross was the manifestation of the promise. His second death was His determination to live in the heavenly dimension.

Are we willing to die to ourselves? Jesus could not achieve the cross in the earthly realm alone. Baptism and Gethsemane had to happen first. Are our thoughts leading us closer to or further from our ascended place? To bring divine order into earthly chaos—to express the DNA of God and bring Heaven into the earth—we must be fully invested in the call.

We have the upper hand. We have the inside knowledge of what is to come. The Holy Spirit hovered over the waters, suspending them from flooding the earth. The conditions of your situation may appear dark and cloudy—past, present, or future—but the Holy Spirit is hovering, watching, guiding, and sustaining the flow.

The earth grew so dark that God destroyed it and started over—for those willing to sacrifice it all. For those willing to wipe the slate clean, God is restoring your life. Some things you can take with you; some things must be left behind. The sacrifice of this season will release a mighty harvest of new life.

CHAPTER 13
A CLEAN SLATE

*E**mbrace your second death and your new sacrifice! God is wiping the slate clean!* Your second death marks your new sacrifice, and God is wiping the slate clean. In this season, the Lord is calling you to lay down what cannot cross into your next dimension, to release what no longer aligns with His purpose for your life. As you surrender, Heaven responds. What once burdened you is being buried, and what God has ordained is being resurrected. This is not the end—it is the divine reset that prepares you for greater covenant, greater clarity, and greater glory.

Noah sacrificed to reestablish the covenant that had been broken by sin and lawlessness. After his sacrifice on the altar, the Lord declared that He would never again curse the ground because of mankind—even with the continued presence of evil. The waters replenished the earth's resources, and the fruitfulness of the ground was sustained through dirt, planting, and water.

Genesis 8:18–22 declares:

> "So Noah came out, together with his sons and his wife and his

> sons' wives. All the animals and creatures—one kind after another—came out of the ark. Then Noah built an altar to the LORD, and taking some of all the clean animals and clean birds, he sacrificed burnt offerings on it. The LORD smelled the pleasing aroma and said in His heart: 'Never again will I curse the ground because of humans, even though every inclination of the human heart is evil from childhood. And never again will I destroy all living creatures.' While the earth remains, seedtime and harvest, cold and heat, summer and winter, day and night shall not cease."

Man's agenda is to be fruitful, multiply, subdue, and fill the earth—to take dominion. He would not have to take dominion if there were no opposing force. In this new place God is preparing, a new sacrifice and a new covenant are required. The aroma of your sacrifice will bring change to your life and to the lives of those connected to your purpose.

Ephesians 1:3–5 declares:

> "Praise be to the God and Father of our Lord Jesus Christ, who has blessed us in the heavenly realms with every spiritual blessing in Christ. For He chose us in Him before the creation of the world to be holy and blameless in His sight. In love, He predestined us to be adopted as His sons through Jesus Christ, in accordance with His pleasure and will."

Jesus was always the mediator before He had to redeem us. Hebrews 9:15 states,

> "Therefore Christ is the mediator of a new covenant, so that those who are called may receive the promised eternal

> *inheritance, now that He has died to redeem them from the transgressions committed under the first covenant."*

> *"The testimony of Jesus is the spirit of prophecy."*
>
> — REVELATION 19:10

He is the Word over us fulfilled. It was God's plan from the beginning to send His Son to die on the cross for mankind's sins. God is omniscient—He knew everything. Before laying the foundations of the world, He already knew that man would sin and perish without His help. Therefore, He prepared a plan of salvation—a way for us to be reconciled to God through His Son Jesus Christ, our only Mediator and Intercessor.

Ephesians 3:9–11 declares:

> *"To make plain to everyone the administration of this mystery, which for ages past was kept hidden in God, who created all things. His intent was that now, through the church, the manifold wisdom of God should be made known to the rulers and authorities in the heavenly realms, according to His eternal purpose that He accomplished in Christ Jesus our Lord."*

God not only prepared the plan of salvation but also made it known to man. From the very beginning, He began revealing it in His Word. The main theme of the Bible is Jesus Christ. From the start, we see the promise of a Savior. When Adam sinned, God told him He would provide a Savior who would crush the serpent's head.

The Bible was written to build our faith so that we can see Jesus as the fulfillment of God's plan.

- We have witnessed
- We witness
- We testify

CRYSTAL LOVE

When we testify of Jesus on earth, the Kingdom of Heaven is coming. Our speech and agreement are covenant. Our voice, prayer, and proclamation are where the fight is won. We were witnesses from the beginning of time. There is no age in the Holy Spirit. We feel confirmation because we were there before. We are aware of what is, what was, and what is to come.

It is sometimes difficult to live here because we know there is more. Jesus, in His divinity, had to go through the trenches and formalities of the earthly realm. We all experience the birthing pains of something inside us that God placed there. This assignment—this mantle—must be released in the earth. Whether anyone yields to it or not, it is still there. It becomes uncomfortable when it is not released. It grows until it is expressed, and until that happens, life feels incomplete.

Paul said, "When I go to do good, evil is always present." Why? Because there is a war in our members—a tension between spirit and flesh. This is the battle of the two worlds. Jesus Himself said you cannot serve two masters; you will love one and hate the other.

Paul said, "When I go to do good, evil is always present." Why? Because there is a war in our members—a tension between spirit and flesh. This is the battle of the two worlds. Jesus Himself said you cannot serve two masters; you will love one and hate the other.

This is the painful reality for those chosen for dual existence—you cannot be neutral. There is no in-between. The cost of your calling is clarity.

But clarity brings confidence. Confidence comes from knowing you were not born to blend in—you were born to build, to establish God's Kingdom, to judge rightly, to witness boldly.

We are a witness. Heaven is counting on your testimony.

> *"And they overcame him by the blood of the Lamb and by the word of their testimony..."*
>
> — REVELATION 12:11

Witnessing is not just about what you say—it is about what you have seen. When you open your mouth, you release Heaven into the earth. That is why the enemy attacks your voice—because your words carry weight. They are evidence in the courts of Heaven. The Holy Spirit trains you to speak what Heaven says. He teaches you how to declare truth even when you are surrounded by lies. He reminds you that your position in the spirit is not dictated by your situation in the natural.

You are seated in heavenly places (Ephesians 2:6).

When you testify, you are not merely telling your story—you are reinforcing God's verdict over your life. When you are chosen, the Word of God is spoken, created, and branded in your heart and in your DNA, so that when the enemy tries to come against you and stop the plan of God, he cannot—because it is written, and it cannot be erased. If sin were not the factor, then the Bible would simply be another history book. The Word of God is our sword; it is what we use to fight. It is needed for cleansing and revelation. It is through the Word of God that we know who Jesus Christ is, His redemptive work in reconnecting us to God, and the working power of the Holy Spirit. This, therefore, grants us the right to disciple others into the Kingdom of God, to live blameless until the final judgment.

When we think about the court system and how it is structured, here is a brief overview: the courtroom has a judge, a plaintiff, a defendant, witnesses, and sometimes jurors. The courtroom reporter records everything spoken audibly, and at times an artist captures the scenes visually. The evidence is then presented to bring clarity to what happened and to help the judge make a sound decision.

The difference between the earthly courthouse and the heavenly realm is that God already knows what is right and wrong and what decisions should be made in every situation. The cases presented in the courtroom of Heaven are set to bring order and judgment to every matter. Judgment is needed for both the good and the bad, ultimately to rightly and fairly separate the two. It reveals that the sacrifice of Jesus Christ was sufficient for every case and every accusation. The only one bringing accusations before the courts is Satan.

God established this system to benefit us. Jesus represents those who have placed their trust in Him before God's throne of grace. He mediates for us much like a defense attorney mediates for his client, saying to the Judge, "Your honor, my client is innocent of all charges…"

> "The Lord said to Satan, "Have you considered My servant Job? For there is no one like him on the earth, a blameless and upright man, fearing God and turning away from evil." Then Satan answered the Lord, "Does Job fear God for nothing? Have You not made a hedge about him and his house and all that he has, on every side? You have blessed the work of his hands, and his possessions have increased in the land."
>
> — JOB 1:8-11

> "Then he showed me Joshua the high priest standing before the angel of the Lord, and Satan standing at his right hand to accuse him. The Lord said to Satan, 'The Lord rebuke you, Satan! Indeed, the Lord who has chosen Jerusalem rebuke you? Is this not a brand plucked from the fire?'"
>
> — ZECHARIAH 3:1-2

> "Who will bring a charge against God's elect? God is the one who justifies."
>
> — ROMANS 8:33

In order for dual citizenship to function—citizenship in both the Kingdom of Heaven and the earthly kingdom—we must be fully surrendered and yielded to the Heavenly Kingdom. We have freedom and liberty in Christ Jesus, with full authority and full rank, but only when we are surrendered. That authority was taken from us in the beginning because of disobedience. We defiled the consecrated lifestyle. The relationship that had been established was destroyed. The covenant, the seal, the connection—was broken. And in order to reestablish it, certain formalities must take place for restoration and for that covenant to be sanctioned again.

Think about it in earthly terms: if your license is suspended, there is usually a fine. You receive notices to pay, and if there is no response, the fees accrue. There is a consequence for the violation that caused the suspension. Likewise, there was a consequence for the violation of disobeying God and breaching the covenant established from the beginning.

We can no longer afford to breach our covenant with God because of our earthly connections. Too often, we compromise our agreement with God to maintain peace with people and relationships on earth. But when God instructs us to connect with someone, to disconnect from certain places, to leave a job, or to shift directions, we must be obedient. This is why we have the Holy Spirit—to lead, guide, and direct us. When we listen, we avoid pitfalls. We avoid careless mistakes and wasted time that come from ignoring divine instruction.

The earth is cursed. We were formed from the earth. There is nothing man can do to preserve the earth itself—it is wasting away. It serves its purpose for this moment only. The only reason the earth still exists is because God has allotted us time to expand the Kingdom of Heaven and preserve His people. This is our window to bring people into the ark before final destruction—before the complete breakdown of a world full of death, decay, and sin. What is holding the earth together right now is God's grace upon His people, His seed, His children.

So when we put on the armor of God, we are stepping into a war zone. It is like when soldiers go to battle and the enemy has infiltrated their camp. They must defend the nation, retrieve what belongs to them, and rescue the wounded. Someone must cover them. Someone must go in and get those who are defenseless, surrounded, or isolated. We are fighting for territory.

The twelve tribes of Israel were given land to conquer. The land was already theirs—they just had to go and possess it. When God says something is yours, you must believe it before you see it, before you touch it. When God gives you a vision, a dream, or a prophetic word, it is already established in Heaven. It is not something you must create from scratch. He shares it with you so that you can come into agreement with it and bring it into the earth.

A divine word comes with divine instruction to pull every piece of the vision into place. That is how establishment happens. Out of the mouth of two or three witnesses, His word is established. God speaks it to you, then He connects you to the people the Holy Spirit leads you to. These are the ones who help fulfill the vision. Together, you begin building on the foundation of the word God gave. And because we have one Spirit—the Holy Spirit—someone else filled with that same Spirit will bear witness to what He told you. They will connect with the vision, and together, it will flourish.

We have the capabilities through the Holy Spirit to release Heaven on earth while living in two worlds. In Genesis 1, the Spirit hovered over the waters, waiting for the Word, and the moment God spoke, order began to form. This pattern continues today. The Spirit still hovers, waiting on your agreement, and when you open your mouth and align with what Heaven is saying, you release divine order into chaos. Your voice becomes a tool of transformation. Your prayer becomes a courtroom petition. Your obedience becomes the evidence. You have the authority to bring Heaven into your home, your city, and your generation.

> *"Let Your kingdom come, Your will be done, on earth as it is in Heaven."*
>
> — MATTHEW 6:10

This is not just a prayer—it is your assignment. You are called to fulfill your chosen position. To be chosen means to be entrusted. You are entrusted with the dual responsibility of living in the earth while releasing Heaven. It is not an easy life, but it is an empowered one. You live in two worlds to fulfill one purpose: to glorify the One who created you, to bring order to what has been disordered, to proclaim the justice, mercy, and love of God, and to walk in dominion while pointing all things back to Him.

You were chosen to live in two worlds, and you were never meant to live them alone. Living from Heaven and operating on earth is a dual assignment that requires you to understand how to translate Heaven into earth. That is where the Holy Spirit comes in. He is your interpreter, your counselor, and your trainer. He takes the mind of God and reveals it to you so that you do not live by assumption but by revelation. Without the Holy Spirit, your earthly life becomes guesswork. With Him, your spirit knows how to navigate warfare, how to speak the language of Heaven, and how to interpret the signs of the times.

Jesus modeled this for us. He operated in the earth but never lost His connection to Heaven. Even in Gethsemane, while His flesh was overwhelmed, His spirit remained surrendered, saying, "Not My will, but Yours be done." That is the posture of a dual dweller. You can feel the pain of the earth and still submit to the plan of Heaven.

When the courts of Heaven are in session, we must remember that we have an Advocate. Every time the accuser tries to speak against your destiny, your High Priest, Jesus Christ, intercedes. He does not merely defend you; He presents the blood that silences every accusation. And what does the blood say? "It is finished." Even when your earthly reality screams "guilty," the blood still pleads your case.

This is why you cannot live by what you feel or see—you must live by what has already been spoken in Heaven. When you operate as one seated in heavenly places, you see your trials through a different lens. You do not pray from defeat; you pray from dominion. Many fear judgment because they misunderstand it. God's judgment is not punishment for the saved—it is vindication. It is restoration. It is God revealing what is rightfully yours.

CRYSTAL LOVE

> *"The Lord arises to judgment—to save all the humble of the earth."*
>
> — PSALM 76:9

Judgment is Heaven declaring, "This one belongs to Me." It is God weighing the accusations of the enemy and proclaiming, "Case dismissed. Covered in the blood." You were made for dominion. The fall of man did not cancel your calling; it revealed your need for a Savior. Now, because of Christ, we are no longer merely dust—we are divine breath with a mandate. Our assignment is not survival; it is dominion.

> *"You have made him to have dominion over the works of Your hands; You have put all things under his feet."*
>
> — PSALM 8:6

What is under your feet? Fear. Shame. Confusion. Sin. Everything that wars against your divine identity must bow. The blood speaks louder than your mistakes, and the Spirit speaks louder than your trauma. You were born to subdue chaos, to bring light into darkness, to bring Heaven into homes, and to speak peace into storms. As born-again believers, we must understand that Heaven is our home, and earth is the location where we walk out our assignment. Let this sink in: Heaven is not just where you are going—it is where you are seated right now (Ephesians 2:6). This is why Jesus said,

> *"Rejoice, you who dwell in Heaven!"*
>
> — REVELATION 12:12

Even while walking on earth, you can live from your true address. That is how you conquer sin, temptation, accusation, and fear. You live from the seat you have been given, not the soil you came from.

This means you no longer operate from trauma, past pain, or previous mistakes. You operate from position, power, and the promise that you were chosen before the foundation of the world, sealed with the Holy Spirit, and written in the Book of Life. It may feel difficult at times to adjust to this earthly abode because you were never designed to fit into just one world. Your soul feels the pull of Heaven while your flesh experiences the pressures of the earth. This is why there is a war inside of you. This is why you feel misunderstood—because you were not created to be understood by the world but to transform it. God trains you to speak Heaven's language. Your voice matters. Your voice is the legal entry point through which Heaven's rulership manifests. When you speak in agreement with God, Heaven moves. You live between realms, not for confusion but for purpose. Only someone who walks in both can bring them into alignment.

We must understand that we were always Plan A. The devil may have been in the earth before you, but you were always Heaven's intention. God gave dominion to humanity, not angels. The enemy may have been cast down to the earth, but you were sent here to reign in it.

"The Spirit of God hovered over the waters..."

— GENESIS 1:2

That same Spirit now hovers over your life, waiting for your agreement, your surrender, and your voice. So speak. Command order. Speak light into darkness. Release the Word of the Lord into chaos. When you open your mouth as a citizen of Heaven, you remind hell that its reign is temporary.

There was a divine exchange when Jesus died to free you from sin. Now you live to release that freedom into the earth. There is always an exchange—His sacrifice demands your surrender, and His Spirit empowers your obedience. You cannot serve two masters. You cannot straddle the fence. You cannot live as a slave to sin and a servant of righteousness. So choose. Choose Heaven. Choose purpose. Choose to live in two worlds—but to build for only one. You were chosen to live in two worlds. Live well. Rule well. Speak boldly. You are the living evidence that the Kingdom of Heaven is not just near—it is here.

CHAPTER 14
THE FULL EXPRESSION OF THE HOLY SPIRIT

The Holy Spirit is revealed in Scripture through many dimensions, each displaying a unique aspect of His power and purpose in the life of the believer. His *fruit* transforms us inwardly so that our character reflects Christ. His *spiritual gifts* empower us supernaturally to carry out God's work in the earth. Through the *five-fold ministry*, He appoints leadership offices that equip and mature the body of Christ. And in the *seven spirits of God*, we see the fullness, depth, and complete expression of who He is. Together, these manifestations reveal the richness of the Spirit's ministry and His desire to work in us, through us, and for the glory of God. Let's explore each area together.

THE FRUIT OF THE SPIRIT

The fruit of the Spirit refers to a set of virtues that are produced in the life of a Christian who is indwelt by the Holy Spirit. These virtues (high moral standards) or qualities are listed in Galatians 5:

> *"But the fruit of the Spirit is love, joy, peace, forbearance,*

kindness, goodness, faithfulness, gentleness and self-control. Against such things there is no law."

— GALATIANS 5 22-23

Only the Holy Spirit can produce these; the works of the flesh are plural while the fruit is one.

It's time for us to walk in the fullness of God and the fullness of the Holy Spirit—the Spirit who lives within us—so that we can truly experience the manifold wisdom of God. Through Him, we can encounter the wonderful counsel of God, submit to His Lordship over our lives, and embrace everything He has prepared for us. The heavenly experience is not something we must wait for; we can live it here on earth.

We don't have to be limited by this world, because God Himself dwells in us. When we allow Him to take over—when we recognize the Holy Spirit as a person, as our Helper, our Guide, and our Friend—we realize that He is not separate from us but united with us. He is in us, and we are one with Him.

It has always been God's design for His people to live fruitful lives. Scripture says, "Be fruitful, and multiply, and replenish the earth." The Holy Spirit produces fruit in us—fruit that remains, fruit that prospers, fruit that reflects Christ. Yet it is a choice: we must decide whether or not we will allow the Spirit to guide our lives.

When we surrender to Him, we no longer fall prey to the consequences of our sinful nature. Instead, we yield to the Spirit who makes us holy. The Bible declares, "Be holy, for I am holy." It is the Spirit who stirs our desire to walk in holiness and equips us to be fruitful in every good work for the sake of Christ.

Choosing to produce the fruit of the Spirit keeps us from walking in the desires of the flesh. Paul describes those sinful desires in Galatians 5:19–21. But those who belong to Christ choose instead to live by the Spirit and invite Him to lead every part of life. In moments of temptation and vulnerability, we will not be satisfied with compromise. We will long to walk in the higher fruit of the Spirit: love, joy, peace, patience, kindness, goodness, faithfulness, gentleness, and self-control. Our pursuit will be maturity in these qualities, which flow from the Spirit's nature. This is not something we can achieve by our own understanding. It comes by revelation—by knowing the Holy Spirit personally, by learning His nature and character, and by remaining sensitive to His leading.

We must be careful not to confuse our emotions with His voice, for our flesh resists His direction. There is always a battle within: the sinful nature fights against the Spirit. But when we choose to follow the Spirit, His character becomes evident in us. These traits are the very nature of Jesus Christ Himself. They are the evidence of growing in the Spirit and living in close fellowship with God through Christ. There is no good thing in the flesh. The sinful nature desires to do evil, which is the opposite of what the Holy Spirit wants and desires. These are two opposing forces that will always be at odds with each other.

It is God's design and intention for us to walk daily in obedience to the Holy Spirit. We are not under the law, which is the law of Moses. Jesus came to fulfill the law, and we are under grace—God's grace and mercy that has been released to us, giving us the ability to walk in freedom and liberty, for Christ has made us free. The results of walking in the sinful nature lead us down an unhealthy path: sexual immorality, impurity, lustful desires, idolatry, sorcery, hostility, quarreling, jealousy, anger, selfish ambition, dissension, division, envy, drunkenness, wild parties, and other sins of that nature. These are the qualities of those who choose to yield to the sinful nature, and this is not what God desires. When we continue in the lust of the flesh, the kingdom of God will not be our inheritance. We have to make a decision about what we are going to produce. Are we going to live by the Spirit, or are we going to suppress the nature that God originally ordained and walk in the flesh?

Can you flow in all of the fruit of the Spirit? *Yes.* When the Holy Spirit fully controls your life, you will produce all of these graces. The first three, love, joy, and peace, concern our attitude toward God. The second three, which are long-suffering, kindness, and goodness, deal with social relationships, and the third group describes principles that guide our conduct, which are faithfulness, gentleness, and self-control. The fruit of the Spirit is produced in the life of a believer as they grow in their relationship with God and allow the Holy Spirit to work in their lives. It is a result of the inner transformation that takes place when a person becomes a follower of Jesus Christ. Here is a brief explanation of each of the nine fruits of the Spirit: character traits produced in the life of a believer by the Holy Spirit.

> *"By their fruit you will recognize them. Do people pick grapes from thornbushes, or figs from thistles? Likewise, every good tree bears good fruit, but a bad tree bears bad fruit. A good tree cannot bear bad fruit, and a bad tree cannot bear good fruit. Every tree that does not bear good fruit is cut down and thrown into the fire. Thus, by their fruit you will recognize them."*
>
> — MATTHEW 7:16–20

How do you know the essence of a person? The fruit. Why do you think God has it labeled the fruit of the Spirit? The Holy Spirit is there. The seeds of the fruit are there when you receive His Spirit, but you have to water and allow life experiences and the Word, from which spiritual development happens; God uses everything.

In developing a relationship with God, He gives us room to grow. This is why, after we give our lives to Christ, and after we invite Him to be Lord over our lives, we acknowledge Jesus Christ as our Savior and receive the redemptive act that was done on the cross to wash us of our sins permanently and to redeem us back to our Father. He did not ever want us to try to keep ourselves. He said He came for the lost. He came to save the lost. He came to preserve us until the day of redemption, and the greatest way to do this—to make sure that this plan follows all the way through—is that He gives us Himself. He showed us how to grow and reproduce after our own kind. All of it goes back to when He created the world—everything was a process.

He did not allow man to come forth without anything to do. Even before sin came into the world, He did not have anyone to attend to the productivity that the earth was getting ready to produce. This is why He did not allow rain to fall, so it was held back because He needed someone to watch over and keep the vegetation.

Our intercessor, Jesus Christ, is watching over us to make sure that we continue to produce fruit. We are doing our part by making sure we water ourselves with the Bible, the Word of God. We are armored with the armor of God to ensure that nothing will hinder our growth. There are many Scriptures in the Bible to make us aware of the battle that we are in and help us to understand that we must protect ourselves; the Bible says to guard our hearts with all diligence, for out of it flow the issues of life. We are going to have issues in this world, but the fruit of the Spirit helps us to react and respond to life's issues by producing fruit, by expanding and growing, and by releasing whatever He requires for us to release through and by His Spirit only, not by the works of the flesh.

You know, there is a dual process that He is doing: not only is He helping us walk through our own personal issues, but He's also given us practical strategies from heaven as to how to be His template in the earth—where we can go through things by trial and error, learn, and still grow. Because the Bible says that all things work together for the good of those who love the Lord and are called according to His purpose. Because we love Him, we're going to keep His commandments. We're going to walk according to His Word and His purpose for our lives, and then other men will know that we are His disciples by the love we show—the fruit of the Spirit being expressed in the earth.

So, it's not only going to produce fruit in our own lives, but it's going to be fruitful for other people, too, that they will glean from the fruit that we are producing as a body.

So, we have this big garden that is within, flowing without, which will cause other people to come to Christ. It's productivity inside and outside—spread abroad. We are the eyes, ears, feet, hands, and mouth of God through the person of the Holy Spirit. It is very unlikely that, when we totally yield to the promptings of the Holy Spirit, our lives will produce the same results as they did prior to total surrender.

When you are hired for a job, you usually have to, prior to even applying, possess some type of skills, whether it be through an internship, a degree obtained at a college, or trade school training to prepare you for the job. There are some instances where you have no experience or knowledge of the skills or talents needed to fulfill the job, but there is what you call "no experience needed; training provided."

The thing about our relationship with God and our development into knowing what we already have can be mind-boggling. Having a natural ability to live life in a more efficient and effective way, and not knowing that you have it, is a realization that is prevalent among many people in this world and in the church.

I don't know if we are aware of this, but there are people in leadership positions, even within the five-fold ministry, who are not confident in their God-given abilities and use them as shallow reference points. Some never fully walk in the fullness of God.

This also involves coming to the understanding that we knew God in the Spirit, so when we are born again, we are getting reacquainted with who God made us. This is why we can only know Him and fellowship with Him in spirit. If not, it would be like speaking a foreign language without an interpreter. The interpreter of spiritual things is the Holy Spirit. This is why we cannot live without Him.

Life is limited when we choose to live without the Spirit of God in His full capacity. God will not be in competition with anyone. It is a total agreement that we must come into in order to walk out life with Him. Life is full of interruptions, but the flow will never stop.

We develop a relationship with God and growth in faith by establishing a covenant with God, sacrificing time to have greater intimacy with our Father, and walking out this life in obedience to His divine will for our lives.

THE HOLY SPIRIT EXPLAINED

"I am the vine; you are the branches.
If you remain in me and I in you, you will bear much fruit;
apart from me you can do nothing."

— JOHN 15:5

There is a guarantee that we will extensively grow when we stay connected to God because He is eternal and there is no end to the revelation that He releases to us. We can't fully handle the totality of who He is beyond this earthly realm, but our heavenly seated place will allow us to receive, perceive, and understand as our desire after Him persists.

1. *Love:* An unconditional, selfless love that seeks the good of others above oneself.
2. *Joy:* A deep sense of happiness and contentment that comes from knowing and serving God.
3. *Peace:* A sense of inner calm and tranquility that comes from trusting in God's sovereignty and provision.
4. *Forbearance (patience):* The ability to endure difficult circumstances and people with grace and kindness.
5. *Kindness:* An attitude of generosity and compassion towards others, even in difficult situations.
6. *Goodness:* A moral excellence that seeks to do what is right and just.
7. *Faithfulness:* A loyalty and commitment to God and to others.
8. *Gentleness:* A humble and gentle spirit that seeks to serve others and put their needs before one's own.
9. *Self-control:* The ability to restrain one's own desires and impulses, and to remain disciplined and focused on God's purposes.

The Bible talks extensively about the fruit of the Spirit. The fruit of the Spirit refers to a list of virtues that are seen as the byproduct of the Holy Spirit working in the lives of believers. These are actually the result of the Holy Spirit working in us. In this book, we will look at each of these virtues and study the biblical references associated with them.

ATTITUDE TOWARDS GOD

The first fruit of the Spirit mentioned is *love*. What does the Bible say about love?

> *"Love is patient, love is kind. It does not envy, it does not boast, it is not proud. It does not dishonor others, it is not self-seeking, it is not easily angered, it keeps no record of wrongs. Love does not delight in evil but rejoices with the truth. It always protects, always trusts, always hopes, always perseveres. Love never fails."*
>
> — 1 CORINTHIANS 13:4–8

While this is a summary of what love is, it expands far beyond this description. The Bible teaches that God is love, and that we should love both God and our neighbors. While this virtue may seem a bit difficult, especially as it pertains to the dealings with others, fruit is meant to be shared to others. It's more of a blessing to give than to receive. We are given and shown the love of Christ, not just to keep it to ourselves but to give to others. God's love is expansive and it was not given sit, but to spread like wildfire and cause others to experience His love one on one.

> *"It is more blessed to give than to receive."*
>
> — ACTS 20:35

Jesus came to earth "not to be served, but to serve, and to give his life as a ransom for many" (Matthew 20:28). Giving reflects our likeness to Christ and this gives us a way to show the word the gospel lived out in its purest for by God's love. As believers this is how we continue to walk out John 3:16 as servants of God living a sacrificial life of releasing His love to others.

Then, we have the fruit of the Spirit of *joy*, which is seen as a natural response to the work of the Holy Spirit in our lives. The Bible teaches that we should be joyful at all times, even when facing difficult situations.

One thing that I love about the joy of the Lord is that it gives you the strength in tough times Nehemiah 8:10. It's something that flows through you that becomes a natural response to life because we allow the Holy Spirit to produce maturity in this area and release it. Things happen to produce happiness, but joy is a supernatural release that no matter what's happening, you will have access not just for you, but for others. It will become contagious when in somber moments a burst of joy can lift burdens and brighten someone's day.

I encourage you to practice exercising the fruit. Though it flows through the Holy Spirit, you can pray in faith in moments where it is really needed for it to be released. This is a part of character development. And soon it will be a natural reaction and sense of being, because it is who you are in Christ Jesus.

The fruit of *peace* is seen as a result of being in a right relationship with God. We are told in the Bible that we should strive to live peacefully with others (Romans 12:8).

> *"If it is to encourage, then give encouragement; if it is giving, then give generously; if it is to lead, do it diligently; if it is to show mercy, do it cheerfully."*
>
> — ROMANS 12:8

SOCIAL RELATIONSHIPS

Patience is seen as the ability to endure difficult situations with calmness and tranquility. The Bible teaches that we should be patient with one another, just as God is patient with us.

> *"With all humility and gentleness, with patience, bearing with one another in love, eager to maintain the unity of the Spirit in the bond of peace."*
>
> — EPHESIANS 4:2–3

Patience, like all the other fruits, develops over time, but sometimes the development comes through situations that require patience to be exercised. We have to use the fruit in order for more to be produced. Fruit grows from a seed that is planted first. The seed was planted at salvation and watered by the Word of God. The watering and developing of this seed is intentional; it's a tending of the garden that has to be consistent in order for the fruit to remain.

> *"Ye have not chosen me, but I have chosen you, and ordained you, that ye should go and bring forth fruit, and that your fruit should remain: that whatsoever ye shall ask of the Father in my name, he may give it you."*
>
> — JOHN 15:16

The next fruit is *kindness*, which is seen as the inclination towards benevolence and generosity. There are many expressions in the Bible of being kind to one another, especially to those who are in need.

> *"Be kind and compassionate to one another, forgiving each other, just as in Christ God forgave you."*
>
> — EPHESIANS 4:32

Goodness is seen as the quality of being morally upright and virtuous. The Bible teaches us that we should be good to one another, especially to those who are in need.

PRINCIPLES THAT GUIDE OUR CONDUCT

Faithfulness is seen as being loyal and committed to a cause or belief. The Bible teaches us to be faithful to God and to one another.

Gentleness is seen as the quality of being calm, humble, and considerate towards others. The Bible teaches us to be gentle with one another, especially with those who are weak.

Self-control/ self-discipline is seen as the ability to control oneself in order to avoid being tempted by sin. The Bible teaches us to exercise self-control in all aspects of our lives, especially in our behaviors and thoughts.

Growing in the fruit of the Spirit doesn't just happen. As you seek to grow in their relationship with God, the fruit of the Spirit will become increasingly evident in their lives. We may use religious antic and cliques but the true substance comes from the Word and God and the producing of Christ's nature in our lives; this is true discipleship.

What is a disciple? A true disciple of God will be a full expression of how the fruit of the Spirit are demonstrated and expressed in the earth.

A FOLLOWER OF CHRIST

Believe in Jesus Christ as your Savior and Lord: The first step towards becoming a disciple is to believe in Jesus Christ as your personal Savior and Lord. This involves acknowledging that you are a sinner in need of salvation and accepting the free gift of salvation through faith in Jesus Christ.

> *"For God so loved the world that he gave his one and only Son, that whoever believes in him shall not perish but have eternal life.*

CRYSTAL LOVE

For God did not send his Son into the world to condemn the world, but to save the world through him."

— JOHN 3:16–17

Repenting and turning away from sin is a continuous act of discipline. Repentance is a crucial step in becoming a disciple. It involves acknowledging your sins, confessing them to God, and turning away from them. This is a lifelong process of growing in holiness and sanctification.

"Repent, then, and turn to God, so that your sins may be wiped out, that times of refreshing may come from the Lord."

— ACTS 3:19

Our outward expression and public declaration of baptism, which expresses your faith in Jesus Christ and your commitment to follow Him as your Lord. It is an outward symbol of inward transformation and is a significant step in becoming a disciple.

"Therefore go and make disciples of all nations, baptizing them in the name of the Father and of the Son and of the Holy Spirit, and teaching them to obey everything I have commanded you. And surely I am with you always, to the very end of the age."

— MATTHEW 28 19–20

It is very important not to stop there when it comes to our furtherance in our walk with Christ. We have to study the Bible daily, meditate, and walk it out daily. The Bible is the Word of God and is the primary source of spiritual nourishment as being disciples of Christ. It is essential for growth in faith and understanding of God's will.

THE HOLY SPIRIT EXPLAINED

> *"All Scripture is God-breathed and is useful for teaching, rebuking, correcting and training in righteousness, so that the servant of God may be thoroughly equipped for every good work."*
>
> — 2 TIMOTHY 3:16–17

Our direct line of daily communication to God is through prayer. Prayer is a vital part of the life of a disciple. It is through prayer that we communicate with God, seek His guidance and wisdom, and grow in our relationship with Him.

> *"But when you pray, go into your room and shut the door and pray to your Father who is in secret. And your Father who sees in secret will reward you."*
>
> — MATTHEW 6:6 (ESV)

We are not in this alone, and God designed the whole body to work together to sharpen each other; this is why it is vitally important for us to join a community of believers. "iron sharpens iron," found in Proverbs 27:17. This is where you can receive support, encouragement, and accountability. This can be through your local church, small group, or other Christian community.

> *"And let us not neglect our meeting together, as some people do, but encourage one another, especially now that the day of his return is drawing near."*
>
> — HEBREWS 10:25

It is our commission to share the good news of Jesus Christ with others. This can be through evangelism, acts of service, or simply sharing your testimony with others.

> *"Then Jesus came to them and said, 'All authority in heaven and on earth has been given to me. Therefore go and make disciples of all nations, baptizing them in the name of the Father and of the Son and of the Holy Spirit, and teaching them to obey everything I have commanded you. And surely I am with you always, to the very end of the age.'"*
>
> — MATTHEW 28:18–20

We are to continue to follow the example of Jesus Christ by living a life of love, humility, service, and obedience to God's will.

> *"To this you were called, because Christ suffered for you, leaving you an example, that you should follow in his steps."*
>
> — 1 PETER 2:21

SPIRITUAL GIFTS

The *spiritual gifts* are found three passages in the Bible: 1 Corinthians 12:1-20, Romans 12:3-8, and Ephesians 4:11-13. Do you know the spiritual gifts that you have? Do you know how to operate them? Can you have more than one?

> *Now about the gifts of the Spirit, brothers and sisters, I do not want you to be uninformed. You know that when you were pagans, somehow or other you were influenced and led astray to mute idols. Therefore I want you to know that no one who is speaking by the Spirit of God says, "Jesus be cursed," and no one can say, "Jesus is Lord," except by the Holy Spirit.*
> *There are different kinds of gifts, but the same Spirit distributes them. There are different kinds of service, but the*

same Lord. There are different kinds of working, but in all of them and in everyone it is the same God at work.

Now to each one the manifestation of the Spirit is given for the common good. To one there is given through the Spirit a message of wisdom, to another a message of knowledge by means of the same Spirit, to another faith by the same Spirit, to another gifts of healing by that one Spirit, to another miraculous powers, to another prophecy, to another distinguishing between spirits, to another speaking in different kinds of tongues, and to still another the interpretation of tongues. All these are the work of one and the same Spirit, and he distributes them to each one, just as he determines.

Just as a body, though one, has many parts, but all its many parts form one body, so it is with Christ. For we were all baptized by one Spiritso as to form one body—whether Jews or Gentiles, slave or free—and we were all given the one Spirit to drink. Even so the body is not made up of one part but of many.

Now if the foot should say, "Because I am not a hand, I do not belong to the body," it would not for that reason stop being part of the body. And if the ear should say, "Because I am not an eye, I do not belong to the body," it would not for that reason stop being part of the body. If the whole body were an eye, where would the sense of hearing be? If the whole body were an ear, where would the sense of smell be? But in fact God has placed the parts in the body, every one of them, just as he wanted them to be. If they were all one part, where would the body be? As it is, there are many parts, but one body.

The eye cannot say to the hand, "I don't need you!" And the head cannot say to the feet, "I don't need you!" On the contrary, those parts of the body that seem to be weaker are indispensable, and the parts that we think are less honorable we treat with special honor. And the parts that

are unpresentable are treated with special modesty, while our presentable parts need no special treatment. But God has put the body together, giving greater honor to the parts that lacked it, so that there should be no division in the body, but that its parts should have equal concern for each other. If one part suffers, every part suffers with it; if one part is honored, every part rejoices with it.
Now you are the body of Christ, and each one of you is a part of it. And God has placed in the church first of all apostles, second prophets,third teachers, then miracles, then gifts of healing, of helping, of guidance, and of different kinds of tongues. Are all apostles? Are all prophets? Are all teachers? Do all work miracles? Do all have gifts of healing? Do all speak in tongues? Do all interpret? Now eagerly desire the greater gifts.

— 1 CORINTHIANS 12: 1-30

For by the race given me I say to every one of you: Do not think of yourself more highly than you ought, but rather think of yourself with sober judgment, in accordance with the faith God has distributed to each of you. For just as each of us has one body with many members, and these members do not all have the same function, so in Christ we, though many, form one body, and each member belongs to all the others. We have different gifts, according to the grace given to each of us. If your gift is prophesying, then prophesy in accordance with
your faith; if it is serving, then serve; if it is teaching, then teach; if it is to encourage, then give encouragement;if it is giving, then give generously; if it is to lead, do it diligently; if it is to show mercy, do it cheerfully.

— ROMANS 12:3-8

THE HOLY SPIRIT EXPLAINED

So Christ himself gave the apostles, the prophets, the evangelists, the pastors and teachers, to equip his people for works of service, so that the body of Christ may be built up until we all reach unity in the faith and in the knowledge of the Son of God and become mature, attaining to the whole measure of the fullness of Christ.

— EPHESIANS 4:11-13

The spiritual gifts in the Bible are enablements—supernatural abilities that the Holy Spirit gives us to carry out the plan of God in the earth. These are gifts that are given, and the Bible says they are without repentance, meaning we can use these spiritual gifts for the edification of the body of Christ, and in this manner, we grow into them. We are trained, we are taught, and we learn how to use them properly so that they can be of benefit to others and to the expansion and forward progression of the church. They give us the ability to live out God's plan more effectively and with greater detail.

We have the spiritual gifts of faith, mercy, teaching, leadership, exhortation, evangelism, healing, interpretation of tongues, knowledge, discernment, discerning of spirits, prophecy, giving, administration, helps, tongues, apostleship, miracles, wisdom, word of knowledge, word of wisdom, serving, and shepherding. We have all of these gifts, and they are used to be a blessing to others. Some people have more gifts than others, but it is not an area or a stance to look down on anybody who has more or fewer gifts. The question that is raised is: are we using the gifts to glorify God? Are we using the gifts to help other people?

All of the gifts are of the same Spirit, which is the Holy Spirit. We are one body, though many parts. We are all baptized by one Spirit, and we are all here to serve one purpose—that is, to spread the gospel of Jesus Christ so that those who are not saved will not be lost but will come into the knowledge of what was done on the cross and walk in a free life, free from the bondage of sin, and walk in the freedom that Christ has given us. It is God's plan for us to unify even as we use the gifts, while also understanding that there is diversity. Many people may have the same gifts, but they operate in them differently. That does not take away from anyone or how they flow.

Some people are celebrated for the giftings that they have, but sometimes this can lead to idolatry, causing people to be lifted up within themselves. We must always remember that this is an enablement of the Holy Spirit. This is not anything we can do within ourselves, and all the glory belongs to God. The gifts of the Spirit don't just begin in the New Testament. We have to reflect on how they appear in the Old Testament, because it is the same Spirit at work in both. All things that happen in the New Testament often began in the Old Testament.

If we look closely, we will see many examples of how before the internalization of the Holy Spirit in the New Testament—before Jesus came to earth, ascended back to heaven, and gave us the gift of the Holy Spirit to live on the inside—the Spirit was still at work. One of those examples is the gift of leadership. Leadership is not merely a natural ability; it is a gift of the Holy Spirit. Moses was a great example of carrying the mantle of leadership. For many years, he carried the burden alone, but after receiving wisdom from his father-in-law, he prayed over the seventy elders, and God's Spirit filled them with the same gift of leadership that Moses had. God put His Spirit on them, and they became strong leaders in Israel as well, which took the load off of Moses.

The Spirit continued to move throughout the Old Testament in many ways. In Micah 3:8, we see that the Holy Spirit gave Micah spiritual power. The Spirit also gave Daniel wisdom, understanding, and right judgment. According to Exodus 35:31, the Holy Spirit gave the ability to teach. When we look at the Old Testament as the foundation of the New Testament, it makes sense that when the Holy Spirit is now indwelling us, our ability is expanded. Because He inhabits us, we are able to move in a different capacity. Both in the Old Testament and in the New Testament, the Holy Spirit was and is effective.

GIFTS OF THE SPIRIT

- *Prophecy*: This is the ability to speak forth God's message with boldness and clarity, often with a focus on the future or on the spiritual needs of a particular group or individual.

- *Serving (Ministry):* Also referred to as "ministering," this gift involves providing service of any kind; it is the broad application of practical help to those in need.

- *Teaching*: This is one who has the unique ability to clearly instruct and communicate knowledge, specifically the doctrines of the faith.

- *Exhortation (Encouraging):* The ability to provide comfort, support, and motivation to others, often through speaking or writing.

- *Giving*: Gifted givers are those who joyfully share what they have with others, whether it is financial, material, or the giving of personal time and attention. The giver is concerned for the needs of others and seeks opportunities to share goods, money, and time with them as needs arise.

- *Leadership/ Administration:* The gifted leader is one who rules, presides over, or has the management of other people in the church.

- *Mercy (Generosity):* Closely linked with the gift of encouragement, the gift of mercy is obvious in those who are compassionate toward others who are in distress, showing sympathy and sensitivity coupled with a desire and the resources to lessen their suffering in a kind and cheerful manner.

- *Word of Wisdom:* This gift describes someone who can understand and speak forth biblical truth in such a way as to skillfully apply it to life situations with discernment.

- *Word of Knowledge:* This is another speaking gift that involves understanding truth with an insight that only comes by revelation from God. Those with the gift of knowledge understand the deep things of God and the mysteries of His Word.

- *Faith*: All believers possess faith in some measure because it is one of the gifts of the Spirit bestowed on all who come to Christ in faith (Galatians 5:22–23). The spiritual gift of faith is exhibited by one with a strong and unshakeable confidence in God, His Word, His promises, and the power of prayer to effect miracles.

- *Healing*: This is the ability to pray for and bring about physical or emotional healing in others through the power of the Holy Spirit.

- *Miracles:* This is the ability to perform supernatural acts that are beyond human explanation, often in order to confirm the truth of the Gospel.

- *Discerning of spirits:* Certain individuals possess the unique ability to determine the true message of God from that of the deceiver, Satan, whose methods include purveying deceptive and erroneous doctrine. The ability to distinguish between truth and error, and to recognize the presence of evil spirits or false teachings.

- *Diversity of tongues:* This is the divine ability to speak in languages previously unknown to the speaker. This gift authenticated the message of the gospel and those who preached it as coming from God. The phrase "diversity of tongues" (KJV) or "different kinds of tongues" (NIV) effectively eliminates the idea of a "personal prayer language" as a spiritual gift.

- *Interpretation of tongues:* A person with the gift of interpreting tongues could understand what a tongues-speaker was saying even though he did not know the language that was being spoken. The tongues interpreter would then communicate the message of the tongues-speaker to everyone else, so all could understand.

- *Helps*: Closely related to the gift of mercy is the gift of helps. Those with the gift of helps are those who can aid or render assistance to others in the church with compassion and grace. This has a broad range of possibilities for application. Most importantly, this is the unique ability to identify those who are struggling with doubt, fears, and other spiritual battles; to move toward those in spiritual need with a kind word, an understanding and compassionate demeanor; and to speak scriptural truth that is both convicting and loving.

It's important to note that not every believer will possess every spiritual gift, and that the Holy Spirit may choose to give some gifts to some people at certain times and not at others. These gifts are meant to be used for the building up of the church and the glory of God, rather than for personal gain or recognition.

THE FIVE-FOLD MINISTRY GIFTS

As mentioned in Ephesians 4:11–13, "So Christ himself gave the apostles, the prophets, the evangelists, the pastors, and teachers, to equip his people for works of service, so that the body of Christ may be built up until we all reach unity in the faith and in the knowledge of the Son of God and become mature, attaining to the whole measure of the fullness of Christ." These are individuals who are called and equipped by God to serve as leaders in the church, to equip and empower the saints for the work of ministry, and to build up the body of Christ.

What is the difference between spiritual gifts and five-fold gifts?

Spiritual gifts are the supernatural abilities that God gives to believers and are given to anyone in the church for the purpose of building up the church and advancing His kingdom, regardless of their position or role. Five-fold ministry gifts are specific roles and functions within the church. The purpose of both the five-fold ministry gifts and spiritual gifts is to build up the body of Christ and advance God's kingdom on earth.

Together, these five-fold ministry gifts work together to equip and empower the body of Christ for the work of ministry and to build up the church. These five gifts are given by God to equip and build up His people for works of service and to advance His kingdom on earth. While not every person is called to one of these specific roles, every believer is called to serve God and others in some capacity and can benefit from the leadership and guidance of those with these gifts.

The five-fold ministry gifts are a vital part of the Christian faith. These gifts are described in the New Testament book of Ephesians and are designed to equip the body of Christ for ministry and to help believers grow in their faith. In this book, we will take a closer look at each of the five-fold gifts and how they function within the church. The five-fold ministry gifts are an essential part of the church community. Each gift is uniquely designed to equip the body of Christ for ministry and to help believers grow in their faith.

These gifts are not just for the leaders of the church but are available to every believer who desires to serve God. By embracing these gifts, we can experience a deeper sense of purpose and fulfillment in our walk with Christ. The Apostle, Prophet, Evangelist, Pastor, and Teacher all work together to build up the church and enable believers to reach their full potential as followers of Christ.

In Ephesians 4:11–16, we see the five-fold ministry gifts. God gives these spiritual gifts to individuals in the church who are on a mission—specifically, to ensure that the message of Jesus Christ is shared and administered properly. When we consider prophets, it's important to distinguish between the office of a prophet and the gift of prophecy. The office of a prophet is a specific calling that God places on someone, an assignment they are set apart to fulfill. In contrast, the gift of prophecy is an enablement—it gives a person the ability to prophesy, but it is not their primary calling.

The five-fold ministry is used to prepare God's people to carry out the work ordained for the body of Christ. This is the ability to serve, as stated in Ephesians 4:12–13:

> *"To prepare God's people for works of service so that the body of Christ may be built up until we all reach unity in the faith and in the knowledge of the Son of God, and become mature, attaining to the whole measure of the fullness of Christ."*
>
> — EPHESIANS 4:12–13

We see here that the foundation of the church is built upon apostles and prophets, with Jesus Christ Himself being the chief cornerstone, according to Ephesians 2:20. If the apostles and prophets were the foundation of the church, the question is: Are we still building the foundation of the church? And yes, we are, because the work of the apostles and prophets continues to this day. Their role was to release the revelation of God and to teach the truth of His word so that the church could grow.

We have the Word of God as our foundation, on which we continue to build and expand the church, and this is done through the work of the Holy Spirit. The five-fold ministry is needed and very active. The five-fold ministry can also be viewed as the government of the church. When everyone works together in unity, we can accomplish far more because we have more people at work.

People are born with these gifts. While the gifts of the Spirit are available to all, the five-fold ministry gifts are used to equip believers so they can function in their spiritual gifts. Now, we know there is a difference between holding an office and working in a spiritual gift. The responsibility of the apostles in the church is to help equip people to work out their ministry. As we look at the Word of God, the Apostle Paul was very prominent in operating in this office. He wrote a great portion of the New Testament, giving detailed instructions on how we are to walk out our call as believers in the body of Christ.

The prophets are God's messengers, releasing His word to God's people and to the church to edify and build up both the church and its leaders. The evangelist is used to preach and teach, spreading the gospel of Jesus Christ with a true heart for discipleship, to fully build and develop other disciples and help new believers grow in their faith in Christ.

The role of the pastor in our local churches is to care for the needs of the people. They also teach and preach, guarding and protecting the sheep to ensure they are nurtured, groomed, and grow into who they are meant to be in Christ. Teachers are given divine revelation on how to express the Word of God, equipping people to learn, receive, and grow in the Word of God so that their lives can be illuminated.

Not everyone has a five-fold gift. We also have the gifts of the Father, which are with us from birth. These are grace gifts, given according to the measure God gives each individual. Then we have the gifts of Jesus Christ, which are the five-fold ministry gifts. Finally, we have the gifts of the Holy Spirit, which are used to build up the church. Everyone's call and position in the body of Christ is important, and all of it is used to glorify God in heaven, draw people to Jesus Christ, and reveal the work of the cross.

The Apostle

The Apostle has a vision and a desire to establish and build up new churches. Apostles are often trailblazers, paving the way for the gospel to reach new frontiers. They are called to be leaders and have a strong sense of authority. The word "apostle" means "sent one." Apostles are people who are sent out by God to pioneer and establish new works or to oversee and care for existing ones. They often have a strong vision for planting churches or other ministries and have a gift for leadership and authority.

The Prophet

The Prophet releases understanding of God's word and a strong sense of discernment. Prophets are called to speak the truth of God boldly, often challenging the status quo. They are gifted with the ability to give insight into current situations, to reveal hidden things, and to call people to repentance. Prophets are people who hear from God and communicate His messages to individuals or groups. They have a gift for discerning the voice of God and bringing clarity and direction to difficult situations. They also have a heart for justice and often speak out against injustice and oppression.

The Evangelist

The Evangelist has the heart for sharing the gospel with unbelievers. Evangelists are passionate about seeing people come to faith in Christ and often have a unique ability to communicate the gospel in a way that is accessible and understandable. They are gifted with the ability to draw people to Christ.

The Pastor

The Pastor has a heart for people and a desire to shepherd and care for them. Pastors are called to be spiritual leaders who provide guidance and support to those under their charge. They are gifted with the ability to provide comfort, encouragement, and a sense of belonging to those they serve. Pastors have a gift for caring for and shepherding God's people. They have a heart for discipleship and nurturing spiritual growth in others. They often oversee a local church or ministry and provide pastoral care, counseling, and teaching.

The Teacher

The Teacher has a desire to impart knowledge and understanding of God's word. Teachers are called to be communicators of truth, gifted with the ability to explain complex spiritual concepts in an easy-to-understand manner. They are gifted with the ability to impart wisdom and knowledge to others, helping believers grow in their faith. Teachers have a gift for communicating biblical truth in a way that is understandable and applicable to others. They have a passion for studying and understanding the Word of God and often have a gift for making complex ideas simple and easy to grasp.

THE SEVEN SPIRITS OF GOD

The topic of the seven spirits of God is mysterious and fascinating. The Bible mentions these spirits in a few places, and their significance cannot be dismissed. We will take a closer look at what the seven spirits of God are, what they represent, and how they can help us today. It is clear that they are important, since they are mentioned in Scripture and are attributed to God.

The "seven spirits" represent the fullness and completeness of God's Spirit, while the gifts of the Holy Spirit enable believers to operate in these aspects of God's Spirit. The seven spirits of God, which are drawn from and represent the Trinity—the Father, the Son, and the Holy Spirit—are revealed throughout Scripture:

- *Revelation 3:1* – Jesus holds the seven spirits of God.

- *John 15:26* – Jesus sends the Holy Spirit from the Father.

- *Revelation 4:5* – The seven spirits of God are symbolized as seven burning lamps standing before God's throne.

- *Revelation 5:6* – The seven spirits of God are the seven eyes of the Lamb, sent out into all the earth, highlighting His omniscience and omnipresence.

So, why are there "seven spirits" of the Holy Spirit in the book of Revelation? The number seven symbolizes perfection and completion, revealing the fullness and completeness of the Holy Spirit—who He is and how His presence can be released and manifested through us. These seven expressions of the Spirit reflect the totality of His power and wisdom, demonstrating the ways in which He operates in the world and in our lives.

The abilities and gifts that we receive through the Holy Spirit—through the seven spirits of God—can be actively expressed in our lives. They guide our flow and help us understand who God has created us to be. The Bible says that "people perish for lack of knowledge" (Hosea 4:6), and now that we are learning about the fullness of what we have in the Spirit, it should inspire a deeper pursuit of God. It should awaken us to who He created us to be and how we can live in His fullness here on earth, becoming more effective because we now have confidence through knowledge and understanding. The Bible says, "With all your getting, get understanding" (Proverbs 4:7).

Therefore, you can pray and ask the Holy Spirit to reveal His fullness to you and to mature you in these areas. The prophecy of Jesus is not empowered or expressed by seven separate spirits; it is empowered by one Spirit—the Holy Spirit—but He is expressed in seven distinct ways. This reveals both the depth and the completeness of His work in the world and in the life of a believer, showing us that the Spirit is not limited but multifaceted, fully capable of operating in perfect harmony with God's will.

So we have the *fullness* and the *enablement*. *Enablement* helps you carry out the fullness of God, and having the *fullness* and completeness of God's Spirit gives you understanding of how to operate in your spiritual gifts. It gives your gifts more definition and effectiveness.

In Revelation 3:1, Jesus "holds" the seven spirits of God. In John

15:26, Jesus "sends" the Holy Spirit from the Father. Both passages point to the role of the Son and the role of the Spirit.

In Revelation 4:5, the seven spirits of God are symbolized as seven burning lamps before God's throne. This picture agrees with Zechariah's vision, in which he sees the Holy Spirit symbolized as "a solid gold lampstand . . . with a bowl at the top and seven lamps on it" (Zechariah 4:2). This is also symbolic of the candlestick that was in the Tabernacle (Exodus 40:24–25).

In Revelation 5:6, the seven spirits are the "seven eyes" of the Lamb, and they are "sent out into all the earth." The seven eyes speak of the Spirit's (and the Lamb's) omniscience, and the fact that He is sent into all the earth speaks of His omnipresence.

Once we identify the "seven spirits" as the Holy Spirit, the question remains: why are there "seven" of Him? The Bible, and especially the book of Revelation, uses the number seven to refer to perfection and completion. John's vision includes a picture of the perfect and complete Holy Spirit. The Spirit of God holds all that is needed to be effective in the earth according to the Word of God.

Isaiah 11:2 also references the Holy Spirit using a seven-fold description:

> *"The Spirit of the LORD will rest on him—*
> *the Spirit of wisdom and of understanding,*
> *the Spirit of counsel and of power,*
> *the Spirit of knowledge and of the fear of the LORD."*
>
> — ISAIAH 11:2

The prophecy is that the Messiah would be empowered not by seven individual spirits, but by the one Spirit, described in seven ways. The Holy Spirit is one, but has seven diverse manifestations, much as God is one but has three distinct Persons: Father, Son, and Holy Spirit.

1. The Spirit of the LORD

2. The Spirit of wisdom
3. The Spirit of understanding
4. The Spirit of counsel
5. The Spirit of might
6. The Spirit of knowledge
7. The Spirit of the fear of the LORD

1. The Spirit of the LORD

This refers to the Holy Spirit, the third Person of the Trinity, who is sent by God to dwell in believers and guide them in their lives. He enables us to have a deeper relationship with God and empowers us to do God's work.

The Spirit of the Lord gives us freedom.

> *"Now the Lord is the Spirit, and where the Spirit of the Lord is, there is freedom."*
>
> — 2 CORINTHIANS 3:17

2) The Spirit of Wisdom

The Spirit of wisdom refers to the Holy Spirit's ability to grant believers insight and understanding into God's plan and purposes for their lives. We are given discernment and the ability to see from a broader perspective and make wise choices. This Spirit gives us insight into who God is and how we can follow His ways. Wisdom is often associated with the fear of the Lord, which means having deep respect and reverence for God so that we follow what He says about wisdom.

The Spirit of the Lord gives us wisdom.

> *"For the Lord gives wisdom;*

From His mouth come knowledge and understanding."

— PROVERBS 2:6

3. *The Spirit of Understanding*

The Spirit of understanding refers to the Holy Spirit's ability to help believers comprehend God's Word and apply it to their lives. It is the ability to grasp the deeper meaning of things. This Spirit enables us to better understand God's Word and His ways. Understanding is often associated with the knowledge of the Lord, which means having an intimate relationship with Him.

The Spirit of the Lord gives us understanding.

> *"For this reason also, since the day we heard of it, we have not ceased to pray for you and to ask that you may be filled with the knowledge of His will in all spiritual wisdom and understanding."*
>
> — COLOSSIANS 1:9

4. *The Spirit of Counsel*

The Spirit of counsel refers to the Holy Spirit's ability to give believers wise guidance and direction in their decision-making. It is the ability to discern the right path to take in order to please God and fulfill His will. This Spirit opens opportunities for us to serve God and others. Counsel is often associated with the mind of the Lord—having an awareness of God's ways and His plans.

The Spirit of the Lord provides us counsel.

> *"I will ask the Father, and He will give you another Helper, that He may be with you forever; that is the Spirit of truth,*

> *whom the world cannot receive, because it does not see Him or know Him, but you know Him because He abides with you and will be in you."*
>
> — JOHN 14:16–17

5. The Spirit of Might

The Spirit of might refers to the Holy Spirit's ability to enable believers to live a victorious Christian life by providing supernatural strength and ability. It is the capacity to overcome obstacles and challenges and to be bold and courageous in our faith journey.

The Spirit of the Lord gives us power.

> *"'But you shall receive power when the Holy Spirit has come upon you; and you shall be witnesses to Me in Jerusalem, and in all Judea and Samaria, and to the end of the earth.'"*
>
> — ACTS 1:8

6) The Spirit of Knowledge

The Spirit of knowledge refers to the Holy Spirit's ability to give believers insight and understanding into spiritual truths and mysteries. It is the ability to know what we otherwise would not know and to interpret the world through a spiritual lens. Knowledge is often associated with the fear of the Lord and the knowledge of His ways—understanding God's truth and His plan for us.

The Spirit of the Lord gives us knowledge.

> *"'These things I have spoken to you while being present with you. But the Helper, the Holy Spirit, whom the Father will*

send in My name, He will teach you all things, and bring to your remembrance all things that I said to you."

— JOHN 14:25-26

We can use resources to gather information, but truly tapping into the fullness of the Holy Spirit requires dependence on Him. Take time to ask the Holy Spirit, sit quietly, and meditate on the Word of God, and you will receive a personal response. Using resources is not wrong, but when you do, pause and pray: "Lord, give me a deeper understanding of this. Reveal something to me that I have not seen before. Show me what You want me to know." Teaching from others can be helpful, but the Holy Spirit may also speak to you personally, one-on-one. If a message completely contradicts the Spirit of God, it did not come from Him, because He will never guide you in a way that is inconsistent with His nature.

7. The Spirit of the Fear of the LORD

The Spirit of the fear of the Lord refers to the Holy Spirit's ability to give believers a deep reverence and respect for God, so that they live in obedience to Him and honor Him in all they do. It is the recognition that God is holy and worthy of our respect and worship. This Spirit enables us to have a deeper relationship with God and walk in obedience to His Word. The fear of the Lord is often associated with wisdom and knowledge, recognizing God's sovereignty and following His ways.

The Spirit of the fear of the Lord gives us a deep reverence for God.

"The fear of the Lord is the beginning of knowledge, fools despise wisdom and instruction."

— PROVERBS 1:7

By embracing the seven spirits of God, we can enter a deeper level of spirituality and experience the peace and joy that come from serving Him. Without reverence, honor, and conviction, we may not even feel the need to seek His wisdom, knowledge, and understanding. If we fail to value who He is—or fail to recognize that He lives within us and has given us abilities—we are likely to misuse or mishandle them.

BIBLIOGRAPHY

American Psychological Association. (n.d.). *Stress and the body*. https://www.apa.org/topics/stress/body#:~:text=Stress%20causes%20the%20body%20to,%2C%20circulatory%2C%20and%20male%20reproduction

AV1611.com. (n.d.). *KJV Bible dictionary: Wind*. https://av1611.com/kjbp/kjv-dictionary/wind.html

Bible Truth Publishers. (n.d.). *The candlestick of pure gold: Exodus 25:31–40*. https://bibletruthpublishers.com/the-candlestick-of-pure-gold-exodus-25-31-40/edward-b-dennett/typical-teachings-of-exodus/e-dennett/la56849

BibleHub. (n.d.). *The role of God in human life*. https://biblehub.com/topical/t/the_role_of_god_in_human_life.htm

BibleStudyTools Staff (Compilers & Editors). (2025, June 17). *15 amazing attributes of God: What they mean and why they matter*. BibleStudyTools.com. https://www.biblestudytools.com/bible-study/topical-studies/15-amazing-attributes-of-god-what-they-mean-and-why-they-matter.html

Biblica. (2011). *The Holy Bible, New International Version*. Zondervan. (Original work published 1978)

Camp, S. (2020, October 9). *Why should I pray if everything is predestined? Red Bluff Daily News*. https://www.redbluffdailynews.com/2020/10/09/why-should-i-pray-if-everything-is-predestined/#:~:text=Prayer%20is%20a%20means%20to,be%20received%20by%20our%20prayers

Christianity.com. (n.d.). *What does the Bible say about darkness?* https://www.christianity.com/wiki/bible/what-does-the-bible-say-about-darkness.html

Christianity.org.uk. (n.d.). *Predestination and free will*. https://www.christianity.org.uk/article/predestination-and-free-will

Church of Jesus Christ of Latter-day Saints. (2017, February). *A two-edged sword*. https://www.churchofjesuschrist.org/study/ensign/2017/02/a-two-edged-sword?lang=eng

BIBLIOGRAPHY

Crossway. (2023, February 26). *10 key Bible verses on spiritual gifts*. https://www.crossway.org/articles/10-key-bible-verses-on-spiritual-gifts/

DeVries, S. (2020, April 4). *Greater than Moses and Elijah. Today Devotional*. https://todaydevotional.com/devotions/greater-than-moses-and-elijah

Douglas, J. D. (Ed.). (n.d.). *The New Bible Dictionary*. Inter-Varsity Press.

GotQuestions.org. (n.d.-a). *The one who was and is and is to come*. https://www.gotquestions.org/the-one-who-was-and-is-and-is-to-come.html

GotQuestions.org. (n.d.-b). *Weaker vessel*. https://www.gotquestions.org/weaker-vessel.html

GotQuestions.org. (n.d.-c). *You are God's*. https://www.gotquestions.org/you-are-gods.html

Haight, D. B. (1980, October). *The keys of the kingdom. Of the Quorum of the Twelve Apostles*. Church of Jesus Christ of Latter-day Saints. https://www.churchofjesuschrist.org/study/general-conference/1980/10/the-keys-of-the-kingdom?lang=eng

Hibermate. (n.d.). *Why does my body temperature go up at night?* https://www.hibermate.com/blogs/news/why-does-my-body-temperature-go-up-at-night

Joseph Prince Ministries. (n.d.). *Understanding the significance of the olive tree and anointing oil*. https://www.josephprince.org/blog/articles/understanding-the-significance-of-the-olive-tree-and-anointing-oil

Kovalevich, D. (2022, July 17). *What is the five-fold ministry? 5 gifts of Jesus Christ*. Flame of Fire. https://www.ffministry.com/blog/what-is-the-five-fold-ministry

LBC Radio. (n.d.). *Where does our body heat come from?* https://www.lbc.co.uk/radio/special-shows/the-mystery-hour/human-body/where-does-our-body-heat-come-from-19472/#:~:text=Answer%3A%20Your%20body%20has%20exothermic,body%20is%20the%20same%20temperature

NASA. (n.d.). *The water cycle*. https://www.nasa.gov/audience/forstudents/k-4/stories/nasa-knows/what-is-the-water-cycle-k4.html

NASA. (2019). *Water in the universe*. https://www.nasa.gov/feature/goddard/2019/water-in-the-universe/

BIBLIOGRAPHY

National Ocean Service, NOAA. (n.d.). *How much of the Earth is covered in water?* https://oceanservice.noaa.gov/facts/how-much-water.html

New Oxford Dictionary. (n.d.). *New Oxford Dictionary.*

Oxford American Writers Thesaurus. (n.d.). *Oxford American writers thesaurus.*

Oxford Languages. (n.d.-a). *Oxford Languages dictionary.*

Oxford Languages. (n.d.-b). *Oxford language dictionary.*

ReasonsForJesus.com. (n.d.). *10 divine attributes of Jesus Christ.* https://reasonsforjesus.com/10-divine-attributes-of-jesus-christ/

Srock, J. (2022, January 21). *Where do the gifts appear in the Old Testament?* Seek the Gifts. https://seekthegifts.com/where-do-the-gifts-appear-in-the-old-testament/

Study.com. (n.d.). *Elohim: Translations and uses.* https://study.com/academy/lesson/elohim-translations-uses.html#:~:text=Elohim%20is%20one%20of%20the,Israel%2C%20whose%20name%20is%20Yahweh

The Blood Transfusion Service. (n.d.). *Functions of blood regulation.* https://www.blood.co.uk/news-and-campaigns/the-donor/latest-stories/functions-of-blood-regulation/#:~:text=The%20blood%20plays%20a%20role,its%20surface%20with%20its%20surroundings

Tithe.ly. (n.d.). *Characteristics of the Holy Spirit.* https://get.tithe.ly/blog/characteristics-of-the-holy-spirit#:~:text=He%20is%20considered%20to%20be,and%20bring%20conviction%20of%20sin

Transport Safety Victoria. (n.d.). *Anchors.* https://transportsafety.vic.gov.au/maritime-safety/recreational-boating/trip-preparation/safety-equipment/anchors#:~:text=Anchoring%20may%20keep%20the%20vessel,anchor%20and%20line%20is%20recommended

US Geological Survey & National Oceanic and Atmospheric Administration. (n.d.). [Joint publication].

Vocabulary.com. (n.d.). *Vocabulary resources.*

About the Author

Crystal Love, a native of Baltimore, is a devoted mother, Elder, and Prophet within the Christian community. She committed her life to the Lord in 1997 at the age of 17 and accepted her call to ministry at 20. With 25 years of ministry experience, Crystal currently serves as an Elder at Kingdom Worship Center in Baltimore, Maryland, under the leadership of Bishop Gregory Dennis and Pastor Tonya Dennis.

Passionate about community service, Crystal volunteers in homeless shelters, teaches at women's transitional homes, engages in outreach and evangelism, and hosts empowerment events designed to uplift and encourage individuals to walk in their God-given callings.

In 2011, she founded Holistic Ministries, which focuses on addressing the comprehensive needs of individuals—spiritual, emotional, social, and physical. Holistic Ministries, Inc. is a parachurch affiliate of Kingdom Fellowship Covenant Ministries, Inc., under the leadership of her spiritual father, Archbishop Ralph Dennis.

Crystal is also the author of several books that promote healing and wholeness. She holds a Bachelor's degree in Pastoral Counseling, equipping her to help others recover through the power of the Holy

Spirit. She is currently pursuing a Bachelor of Science degree with a focus on Religion and Christian Leadership & Ministries. Her ministry reflects her deep commitment to helping individuals discover their purpose in Jesus Christ and expand the Kingdom of God.

> *"When Jesus saw him lie, and knew that he had been now a long time in that case, he saith unto him, 'Wilt thou be made whole?'"*
>
> — JOHN 5:6

ALSO BY CRYSTAL LOVE

Crystal Love's
Book Collection

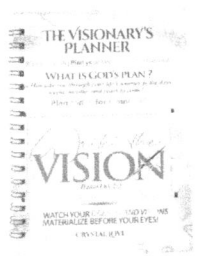  

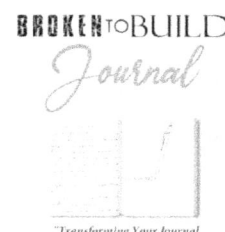